Splendid
Silk Ribbon
Embroidery

*Embellishing
Clothing, Linens
& Accessories*

Splendid
Silk Ribbon
Embroidery

Embellishing
Clothing, Linens
& Accessories

Chris Rankin

Sterling Publishing Co., Inc.   New York
A STERLING/LARK BOOK

Editor: Carol Taylor
Art Directors: Celia Naranjo, Kathleen Holmes
Illustrations: Kay Holmes Stafford
Photography: Evan Bracken
Production: Celia Naranjo
Cover Embroidery: Cathie Bates

Library of Congress Cataloging-in-Publication Data

Rankin, Chris.
    Splendid silk ribbon embroidery : embellishing clothing, linens &
accessories / Chris Rankin.
      p.   cm.
    "A Sterling/Lark book."
    Includes index.
    ISBN 0-8069-4880-9
    1. Silk ribbon embroidery.   I. Title.
TT778.S64R36   1996
746.44—dc20   96-1186
                                            CIP

10 9 8 7 6 5 4 3

A Sterling/Lark Book

First paperback edition published in 1997 by
Sterling Publishing Company, Inc.
387 Park Avenue South, New York, N.Y. 10016

Created and produced by Altamont Press, Inc.
50 College Street, Asheville, NC 28801

© 1996 by Altamont Press

Distributed in Canada by Sterling Publishing
% Canadian Manda Group, One Atlantic Avenue, Suite 105, Toronto, Ontario,
Canada M6K 3E7

Distributed in Great Britain and Europe by Cassell PLC
Wellington House, 125 Strand, London WC2R 0BB, England

Distributed in Australia by Capricorn Link (Australia) Pty Ltd.
P.O. Box 6651, Baulkham Hills, Business Centre, NSW 2153, Australia

The projects in this book are the creations of the contributing designers, who
retain the copyrights to their individual designs. The projects may be reproduced by
individuals for personal pleasure; reproduction on a larger scale with the
intent of personal profit is prohibited.

Every effort has been made to ensure that all the information in this book is accurate.
However, due to differing conditions, tools and individual skills, the publisher cannot
be responsible for any injuries, losses, and other damages which may result from the u
of the information in this book.

Sterling ISBN 0-8069-4880-9 Trade
              0-8069-4881-7 Paper

Contents

Silk Ribbon Embroidery

The Basics

RIBBON EMBROIDERY IS FUN to do and fast to complete. It lends itself to a variety of looks, from tiny, delicate stitches to large, bold strokes. Although it has a natural affinity for flowers (and the vast majority of ribbon work is floral in design), it can be used to portray just about anything. Note, for example, the ladybug and the bumblebees in the photo on page 51, and the grape arbor on page 80. It can also, of course, represent nothing at all, lending the grace and beauty of purely decorative needlework to clothing, pillows, samplers, curtains, linens, and accessories.

Ribbon embroidery has been in and out of favor for centuries, depending on the fashions of the day. Its first heyday was the mid 18th century, when embroidered ribbons bedecked the fashions of the French court. From France it spread to England and then to the British colonies: Australia, New Zealand, the United States, and Canada. It was perhaps most widespread in the 1880s and 1890s, when Victorians' love for decoration was in full bloom. It faded with Victorian fashions. Then, in the late 1980s, ribbon embroidery enjoyed yet another revival, starting in Australia, where needlework has remained an important part of domestic culture. Encouraged by a wealth of silk ribbons now available from Japan, needleworkers both novice and expert have come to love this splendid art.

TOOLS AND MATERIALS
Silk Ribbon

Wonderfully adapted for embroidery, silk ribbon is soft and pliable, willing to lie flat against the background fabric. At the same time, it has enough body to make embroidery very three-dimensional. It's available in an excellent range of colors, from rich jewel tones to extremely subtle shades. Silk ribbons that gradually change from one shade (or even one color) to another can be extraordinarily beautiful in embroidery.

The most common widths of silk ribbon are 4 mm and 7 mm, and in those sizes a wealth of colors is available. The narrower 2 mm ribbon is also popular for more delicate work. Silk ribbon is also available in 13 mm and 32 mm sizes, and while those widths are wonderfully useful, the range of colors is more limited.

Some suppliers carry further refinements. Hand-dyed silk ribbons can produce quite distinctive and individual effects. Bias-cut silk ribbon is available in wider-than-normal sizes: ⅜ inch and ⅝ inch (1 cm and 1.6 cm), for example.

Other Ribbons

Synthetic, silklike ribbons that are made from polyester and rayon can also be used for embroidery, but they are less pleasant to work with and produce different effects. Since they are stiffer, stitches tend to be larger (which needs to be taken into account when planning a design). Most devotees of ribbon embroidery have rather strong preferences for silk. On the other hand, it can be very effective to add small accents of the new synthetics and various other ribbons to pieces that are embroidered primarily in silk.

Double-sided satin ribbon is excellent for large free–form flowers and concertina roses (see page 25).

Organdy ribbon—light, airy, and transparent—can be used for embroidery, as well as for handsome bows, garlands, and streamers tacked to the fabric. Its open weave and delicate look contrast nicely with silk ribbon.

Wire-edged ribbon has thin, flexible wires overlocked along both edges. Wire-edged ribbon has the inestimable value of staying where you put (or bend or shape or twist) it. While it isn't suitable for traditional needlework, it can be shaped into rosettes and streamers that complement the embroidery very nicely.

Grosgrain ribbon is a woven ribbon with a ribbed appearance. Tough and hard-wearing, it traditionally adorned hats and military medals. It's useful on projects that need ties for closures as part of the finishing.

Threads and Flosses

Most silk ribbon embroiderers work part of each design in embroidery thread or floss. Some elements—flower stems and vines, for example—often need a thinner line than ribbon can produce. Various widely available threads work well.

Rayon thread is easy to work with and available in various subcategories, including natesh and Brazilian. Both have a very nice sheen.

Perle cotton is a thick, twisted thread, a workhorse of standard embroidery. Size 8 is the most common for ribbon work pieces.

Silk buttonhole twist is a pretty, lustrous, tightly woven thread that's equivalent to three strands of floss.

Metallic thread is glittery and dressy, whether gold, silver, or copper.

A WOMAN'S WORK:
A GARDEN OF STITCHES
BY ANNIE B. COAN

Coan created an apron shape from appliques of shantung silk, antique silk brocade, taffeta, and linen, then embroidered it in silk ribbon, silk organdy ribbon, satin ribbon, and chenille yarn. Coan's theme is triumph: the movement from darkness and unhappiness into light and joy.

Beads

Beads are beloved by ribbon embroiderers. Available at most craft stores, small seed beads make splendid flower buds, centers for larger flowers, and additions to decorative stitching. Bugle beads—tiny tubular beads—are also eye-catching. Normally, beads are simply sewn onto the background fabric with strong thread.

Needles

The ones you'll use most often are chenille needles and crewel (or embroidery) needles, but others are also useful.

Chenille needle. A large needle with a long eye and a sharp point, it ranges from size 18 to size 24. (The higher the number, the smaller the needle.) Get a packet of assorted sizes and match the ribbon to the eye. Size 18 is most common with 4 mm and 7 mm ribbon; size 20 is large enough for 2 mm ribbon.

Crewel (embroidery) needle. A sharp needle with a long, narrow eye, it's available in sizes 1 to 10. You'll need a packet of assorted sizes to allow you to use the type of floss and the number of stands you choose.

Tapestry needle. Used primarily in cross-stitch and needlepoint, this needle has a blunt end, rather than a sharp point. It's especially useful when working on linen or the kind of evenweave fabric used by cross-stitchers. It's available in sizes 13 to 26. As with chenille needles, size 18 works well with 4 mm and 7 mm ribbons, size 20 with 2 mm.

A large tapestry needle is handy for fiddling with the silk ribbon as you work—spreading it open, shaping it into loops, and so on.

Beading needle. If you plan to add small seed beads to your embroidery, you'll want a needle that's sharp enough to get through the fabric but small-eyed enough to go through the hole in the bead. Any small, sharp needle will do, including a beading needle, available wherever beads are sold. You can also buy bead thread, but any strong thread will do.

When selecting a needle, use the smallest one that will work. Compare the size of the eye and the width of the ribbon: the ribbon should move smoothly through the eye without puckering. As for the size of the needle itself, note that the needle must make a hole in the background fabric large enough for the ribbon to pass through without scraping its sides, thus becoming damaged or frayed.

Fabric

A great many fabrics are suitable for silk ribbon embroidery. Look for a medium weave. An open-weave fabric won't support the ribbon stitches; they'll be floppy and shapeless. If the weave is too tight, you'll have to fight the ribbon through the fabric and will damage it in the struggle. Fabrics that work well include cotton, voile, shantung silk, faille, linen, moire, satin, and embroidery fabrics such as aida and hardanger.

If the embroidery is destined for clothing, whether purchased or homemade, keep several things in mind. First, ironing flattens ribbon stitches and thus essentially spoils the look. Choose a fabric that doesn't need a lot of ironing. Adding a lightweight interfacing to the back of the ribbon area will help prevent puckering around the embroidery and thus

reduce the need for pressing.

Second, the wrong side of ribbon embroidery is a bit messy. When working on a completed garment, you might want to detach the lining in the area you're working on, then reattach it when the embroidery is complete.

Third, silk ribbons vary in washability. (None of them are exactly ducks in water.) If you plan to embroider a garment that must be washed, test the ribbon first. Wet a piece, lay it on a white paper towel, and allow it to dry. Then check for signs of running dye. If the dye has run, choose another ribbon.

Other Necessities

Embroidery hoop. Available everywhere from craft stores to discount marts, an embroidery hoop makes the stitching easier and the results better. Almost all ribbon embroiderers use them. Be sure to remove the hoop from the work when you stop working for awhile, to avoid crushing the embroidery.

Scissors. You'll need a pair of small, pointed, very sharp embroidery scissors for the ribbon and for embroidery threads.

Silk pins. These slender pins are enormously useful for holding ribbons in place. Standard straight pins will make holes in the ribbon that don't go away.

Standard sewing tools. These are the tools that most fabric-oriented folk have lying around the house. (Indeed, they aren't even mentioned in the materials lists for the projects; it's presumed that you have them.) Specifically, you'll often need a tape measure or ruler, standard straight pins, sewing needles (sharps), scissors to cut fabric, scissors to cut paper, and other necessities.

Fleece. Some projects require padding in the process of putting them together. Framed samplers, for example, look much more interesting if some padding is added behind the embroidered fabric during framing. Cotton batting or fleece works well and is available in any fabric store.

TIPS AND TECHNIQUES

Transferring Patterns

The patterns included here can be copied exactly or simply used as suggestions for your own designs. Either way, you'll often want only a few marks on your fabric to guide you: a line for a flower stem and a few dots to help position the petals, for example. In some instances, you may prefer to trace the entire pattern onto the fabric. To do that, place the fabric over the pattern and trace over the lines, using a water-soluble fabric marker, a pencil, or (on dark fabric) a chalk pencil. If there are leftover marks not covered by the finished embroidery, a damp cotton swab is an excellent tool for removing them.

Also available (and widely used) are "disappearing" or "air–soluble" fabric markers, and the marks do indeed vanish of their own accord. However, unless you are in firmer control of your schedule than most of us, the marks can vanish before the embroidery is completed.

Working With Ribbon

Silk ribbon will form creases if given the opportunity, and those creases will inevitably fall in the middle of your best flower, not on the back of the fabric. Some brands of ribbon come wrapped around storage reels. For those that don't, you can cut cardboard tubes from paper towels or bathroom tissue into appropriate lengths and wrap the ribbon around them.

Work with fairly short lengths of ribbon—say, 10 to 14 inches (25.5 to 35.5 cm). The more often the ribbon is pulled through the fabric, the more likely it is to fray.

Threading the Needle

Silk ribbon is easier to work with if you lock it into the needle, rather than leaving a loose tail as you would with embroidery floss. Thread the ribbon through the eye of the needle. Pierce the ribbon end you just threaded with the needle, in the center of the ribbon and about ¼ inch (.5 cm) from the end. Pull the long end of the ribbon, locking the whole strand firmly in place. See Fig. 1.

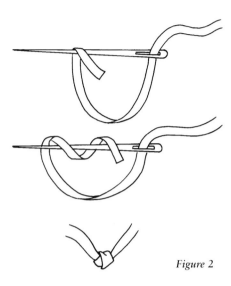

Figure 2

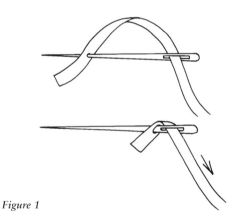

Figure 1

Making a Knot

Before you begin to stitch, knot the end of the ribbon. After threading the needle, lay the long end of the ribbon over the needle; wrap the ribbon around the needle, then pull the needle through to make a knot. See Fig. 2.

Ending a Ribbon

Run the needle under a few stitches on the back of the work, ending the ribbon toward the center of the stitching. For extra security, take the needle through a piece of ribbon on the back, being careful not to disturb your work.

Embroidering Tips

Ribbon can't be treated exactly as if it were embroidery floss, or the results won't be the way you want them. If the ribbon is pulled too tight or allowed to twist when it shouldn't, it will lose its distinctive three-dimensional charm.

As you stitch, use your free thumb to hold the ribbon flat against the fabric, letting it go at the last minute. Try not to let the ribbon twist on the back of the work; that will encourage it to twist on the front on the very next stitch.

MAKING PILLOWS

Pillows make perfect display sites for silk ribbon embroidery, and they're easy to pre-pare. Many shops that sell needlework supplies stock small, round pillows designed for needlework, complete with plain fabric in the center, ready for embroidery. (The pillow on page 94 began life this way.)

If you prefer to cover your own, it's easy to do. Polyester pillow forms are available in any fabric shop in a variety of shapes and sizes, ready to cover with any fabric you choose.

To make a simple pillow, cut a front and a back from the fabric, 1 inch (2.5 cm) larger than the pillow form. Pin front to back right sides together and stitch them together, using a ½-inch (1.5 cm) seam allowance and leaving an 8-inch (20.5 cm) opening in one side. Trim the corners, cutting straight across the points ⅛ inch (3 mm) from the stitching. Turn the pillowcase right side out and insert the form through the opening. Pin the opening closed and edgestitch on the folded edges, or slip-stitch the opening closed by hand. If desired, hand-stitch decorative cording around the edge.

Two interesting variations appear later in the book. The pillow on page 74 has a flange—a flat border around the edge. To add one to your pillow, cut the front and back 5 inches (12.5 cm) larger than the pillow form. Right sides together, stitch front and back with a ½-inch (1.5 cm) seam, leaving an 8-inch (20.5 cm) opening. Turn right side out and press. Topstitch 2 inches (5 cm) from the edge, beginning and ending at the opening. Insert pillow form through the opening and topstitch

the inner area closed, using the zipper foot. Slip-stitch the outer opening closed, or edgestitch around the entire pillow.

A second variation appears on page 78—a pillow covered in printed fabric with a white cotton flap added to showcase the needlework. To add a flap, draw a pattern for the flap, using the shape in Fig. 3 as a guide. Make the pattern 1 inch larger than you want the finished flap to be; note that the long, straight top of the finished flap should be as wide as the finished pillow. Using the pattern, cut a front and back from plain white cotton. Lay the fabric pieces right sides together and stitch around the sides with a ½-inch (1.5 cm) seam, leaving the flat top open. Trim the seam at the point of the flap and turn right side out. Press. When finishing the pillow cover, insert the top of the flap between the front and back of the pillow cover and stitch through all thicknesses.

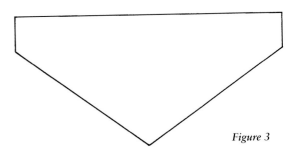

Figure 3

THE PATTERNS

Most of the projects in this book are accompanied by patterns—drawings that indicate which stitches were used to create the design. (The exceptions are projects in which flowers are worked almost at random.) Symbols remain consistent throughout the book; a lazy daisy stitch in the pattern on

Detail of Hot Pink Bomber Jacket, page 32.

page 33 looks the same as one on page 93. A list of symbols on page 29 will serve as a quick guide to what's what.

The patterns are perhaps most useful when used as general guidelines. No two ribbon embroiderers make stitches that are exactly alike. Even if you decide to follow a pattern as closely as possible, your finished product will differ somewhat from the one photographed. That is, of course, part of the charm of handicrafts—they are the unique creations of very individual people.

A WORD ABOUT COLOR

While the materials lists for the projects do specify the type and the size of the ribbons used, they don't specify a particular color or a single manufacturer. Color is a highly individual matter. Tastes and preferences vary widely, as do household decors and facial complexions. Only you know what you like, and only you know which room or which person a project is intended for.

If the designer of a particular piece has worked her roses in mauve and pink and that's exactly what you want, the color photo will see you through. Just select the mauve and pink ribbons that are easiest to find in your area and whose tones please you the most. On the other hand, if you prefer your roses in peach and yellow, or ivory and beige, or even magenta and chartreuse, that's part and parcel of your creativity. It's your project; you get to choose the color.

A Guide to the Stitches

More than a hundred stitches have found their way into silk ribbon embroidery. The same stitches go by various names, depending on the embroiderer, the book, the teacher, or the tea leaves you are consulting at the moment.

Some stitches are used constantly—straight stitch, stem stitch, lazy daisy, and Japanese ribbon stitch, for example. Others, such as Cretan stitch and wave stitch, appear only occasionally but are so handsome and distinctive that they're well worth describing. Some stitches in this guide are old war–horses from the stables of traditional floss embroidery. Others are unique to ribbon work.

Although each of these stitches produces a unique effect, many are interchangeable. For example, a shape can be outlined in backstitch, stem stitch, couching, or whipped running stitch, to name just a few. If a pattern calls for one and you prefer another, feel free to substitute at will.

Backstitch

Normally an outline stitch. Bring the needle up from the back side of the fabric at 1 and go back down at 2, to complete one stitch. Emerge at 3, then go back down at 1 for another stitch. As you work, move the needle ahead under the fabric and come up one stitch length ahead.

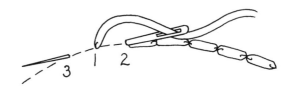

Bullion Knot Stitch

This elegant (but somewhat complex) stitch works well as a filler or an outline. Bring the needle up at 1 and go back down at 2, leaving a loop of ribbon. Bring the needle tip up again at 1. Wrap the loop of thread around the needle five to seven times, or until the knot is as long as the distance between 1 and 2. Carefully pull the needle through both the fabric and the twists. Pull the working ribbon through, holding the twists flat against the fabric. Go down again at 2 and pull firmly.

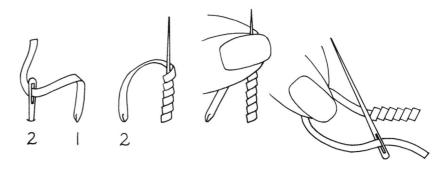

Buttonhole Stitch

Come up at 1. Holding the thread down with your thumb, go down at 2 and back up at 3. Bring the needle over the thread and pull the stitch into place.

Chain Stitch

Come up at 1 and shape the ribbon into a loop. Go back down at 2, one or two threads from 1, and emerge at 3, bringing the needle over the ribbon. Pull until the loop is the desired size. Stitch down at 4 and continue the chain. To end, take the needle down over the end of the last loop.

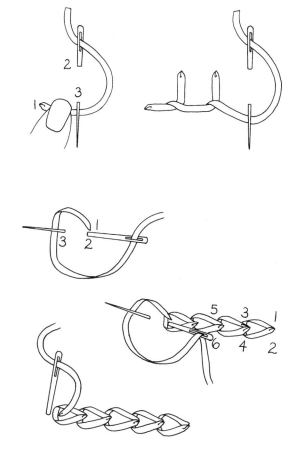

Colonial Knot

Come up at 1. Work the ribbon or thread into a figure 8, as shown in the illustration. Hold the needle vertically and pull the ribbon around the needle. Insert the needle at 2 (close to 1). Hold the knot in place until the needle is pulled through the fabric.

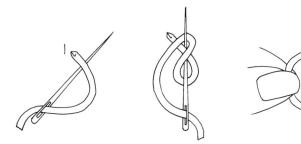

Couching

A classy technique, couching requires two ribbons (or two lengths of embroidery floss) and two needles. Begin with the ribbon that will lie flat. Bring the needle up at 1, at the left side of the area to be covered. Stretch the ribbon over to the right edge and park it. Using your free thumb, hold this ribbon flat.

Bring the second needle up at 1— the first place you want to couch. Bring the needle up and over the flat ribbon and go back down the other side. Repeat until flat ribbon is held in place. At the end of the row, take the first needle back down through the fabric.

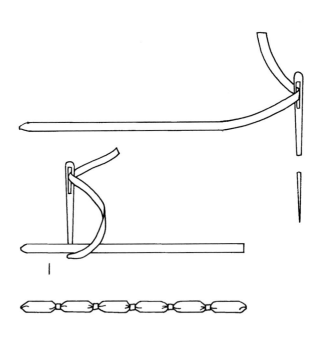

Cretan Stitch

This classy stitch isn't a daily occurrence, but it's worth knowing about. It's worked along two parallel lines. Come up at 1. Go down at 2 and emerge at 3, making a downward vertical stitch and taking the needle over the ribbon. Go down at 4 and back up at 5, making an upward vertical stitch, again taking the needle over the ribbon.

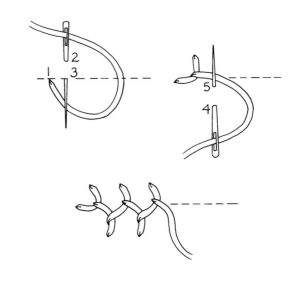

Feather Stitch

Bring the needle up at 1, go back down at 2, and emerge at 3, making sure to bring the needle over the loop of thread. Alternate directions as you work down the line—2 should be to the left of 1, then to the right, then the left, and so on.

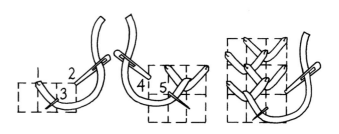

Fern Stitch

Lightly pencil a line the full length of the frond you have in mind. Come up at 1 and go down at 2. Come up again at 1 and go down at 3. Come up again at 1, back down at 4. Come up at 2 and start the next leg of the fern, working along the penciled line as the spine of the fern.

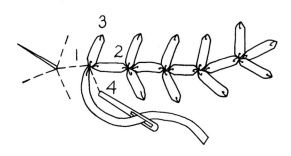

Fly Stitch

Come up at 1 and go down at 2—but don't pull the thread or ribbon tight. Come up at 3, making sure the loop is below the needle. Pull the ribbon toward you to form a V, then insert the needle at 4.

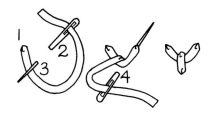

French Knot

Bring needle up at 1 and wrap ribbon once or twice around it. Swing the point of the needle clockwise and take it down at 2 (close to 1). Keep the ribbon wrapped around the needle as you pull the needle to the back of the fabric. Don't pull the knot too tight—ribbon knots should be looser than ones worked with embroidery thread.

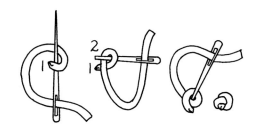

Herringbone Stitch

Working from left to right, come up at 1, go down at 2, and emerge at 3, creating a short horizontal backstitch. Continue the row, alternating from side to side.

An elegant variation of this stitch is to sew small pearls or seed beads in the Vs created at top and bottom of this stitch, using sewing needles and thread. See the Crazy Quilt Vest on page 56.

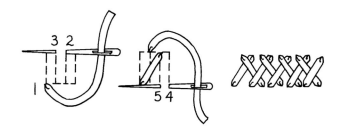

Japanese Ribbon Stitch

Also known simply as "ribbon stitch." Bring needle up at 1 and use your fingers to flatten the ribbon. Just beyond the length of the stitch, insert the needle through the ribbon. Pull the ribbon slowly through the fabric; the sides will curl inward, forming a point. Don't pull the stitch too tight; the curls (the hallmark of the stitch) should remain visible.

When done very loosely, the stitch has a different look: a softer flap at the end.

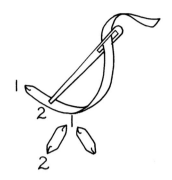

Twisted Ribbon Stitch

Begin a ribbon stitch as usual, but twist the ribbon once before inserting the needle through it.

Lazy Daisy

Aptly named, this is an easy stitch and thus a popular one among sensible embroiderers. Come up at 1 and go down at 2—very close to 1 but a thread or two away, so the ribbon won't be pierced. Pull until the loop is as long as you want it. Come up at 3, with the loop of ribbon below the needle. Pull ribbon through, then go down at 4, to anchor the loop.

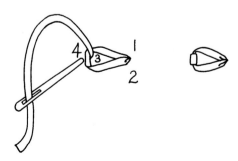

Bullion-Tipped Lazy Daisy

This variation produces a stitch with an extra-long tip. Again, come up at 1 and go down at 2, forming a loop. Come up at 3, with the loop below the needle. But this time wrap the looped ribbon loosely around the needle two or three times. Pull the needle through the wrapped ribbon and the fabric, then go down at 4 to anchor the loop.

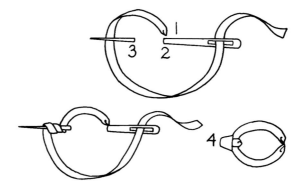

Decorated Lazy Daisy

Make a lazy daisy and then add a straight stitch inside it.

Leaf Stitch

With a pencil, lightly draw a line the desired length of the leaf's spine. Come up at 1 and go down at 2, making a small straight stitch. Bring the needle up at 3 and back down at 4, even with 3; come back up at 5, taking the needle over the ribbon. Go down at 6, to make a small anchor stitch. Continue with the next stitches in the same way, making each set of leaves wider than the previous one.

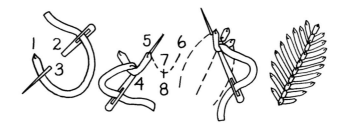

Loop Stitch

Come up at 1, go down at 2, and pull the ribbon through the fabric, leaving a sizeable loop. If you want to be precise in your loops, insert a pencil (pen, straw, toothpick, or large needle) through the loop and pull the loop snug around it. Make the next loop in the same way, moving the pencil to each new loop to keep the sizes uniform.

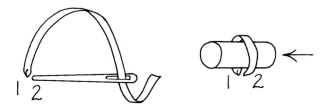

Loop-Stitch Flower

Make a circle of loop stitches, as shown in the illustration.

Montano Knot

This emphatic French knot is the creation of Judith Montano, who has done much to popularize silk ribbon embroidery. Come up at 1 and wrap the ribbon around the needle one to six times. Go back down at 2—as close as possible to 1. As you pull the needle through the fabric, do not hold the ribbon in place, as with other knots; let it go its own abundant way. The stitch should be loose and flowery. Montano knots are especially effective in groups.

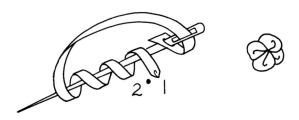

Pistil Stitch

As the name suggests, this stitch is used almost exclusively to make the pistils of flowers. Bring the needle up at 1, allow a short length of thread, and wrap the thread twice around the needle. Go down at 2. Hold the knot in place until the needle is pulled through the fabric.

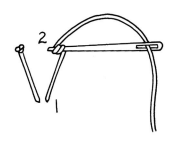

Plume Stitch

This stitch is worked from top to bottom. Come up at 1 and go down at 2, about ⅛ inch (3 mm) lower. Pull ribbon partly through the fabric, creating a loop. Insert a pencil, toothpick, or large needle through the loop to hold it in place. Come up at 3, piercing the first ribbon loop. Go down at 4, ⅛ inch below 2. Continue until the row of loops is the desired length. To end the row, go back down through the bottom of the last loop, taking it down.

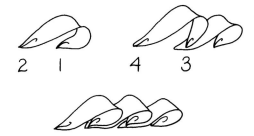

Star Stitch

This makes a good filler and an attractive row, especially for crazy quilt. Come up at 1 and go down at 2, making a straight stitch. Come up at 3 and go down at 4, emerging at 5. This makes the horizontal bar of a cross. Now for the diagonals: 5 to 6 and 7 to 8. Last, make a tiny cross at the center.

Stem Stitch

One of the most-used stitches in ribbon embroidery, this makes a fine flower stem (of course) and excellent vines. It's also invaluable for outlining shapes and can even act as a filler when rows are worked side by side. Draw a line that you want the stitching to follow. Come up at 1; go down at 2 and come back up at the midpoint of the previous stitch.

Straight Stitch

Perhaps the simplest and most versatile of the stitches. Come up at 1 and use your thumb to flatten the ribbon along the length of the proposed stitch. Then take the needle back down at the other end of the stitch and pull gently.

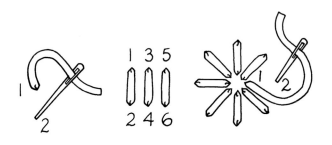

Padded Straight Stitch

Make a straight stitch. Then make a second, somewhat longer straight stitch over the first, for a more three-dimensional effect.

Twisted Straight Stitch

Come up at 1, twist the ribbon once, and go down at 2.

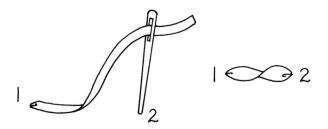

Wave Stitch

Like a spider web rose, a wave stitch uses a string base to weave the ribbon through. To make a base, use embroidery floss and a buttonhole stitch, working the stitches in a circle. Then loop the ribbon through the floss without piercing the fabric, except at the beginning and the end of the stitch.

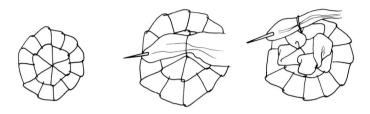

Whipped Running Stitch

First make a running stitch, bringing the ribbon in and out along an imaginary line. To whip it, bring the needle up near the end of the last running stitch. Take the needle under the running stitch, then move on to the next one. Continue until the entire length is wrapped.

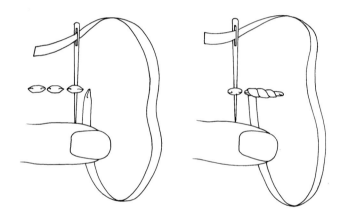

Wrapped Bar

Also called a whipped stitch. Make a straight stitch by coming up at 1 and going down at 2. Come up again near 1. Take the needle under the straight stitch several times, until the bar is completely wrapped. To finish the stitch, go down near 2.

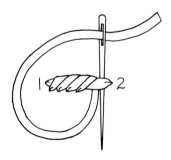

Roses

Flowers are the most popular image in silk ribbon work, and roses appear more often than any other flowers. Here are a few popular ways to work a rose.

BRADFORD ROSE

This handsome rose is from Jenny Bradford, an Australian needleworker and author who has done a great deal to popularize silk ribbon work.

To start, make a loose French knot for the center. Moving clockwise, work three curved wrapped bars around the knot. Change to another color and make four or five more curved wrapped bars around the first group.

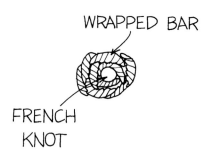

WRAPPED BAR

FRENCH KNOT

CABBAGE ROSE

Unlike the other roses listed here, this variety is formed without a needle and then tacked to the garment. Made with wide ribbon—32 mm silk or 1½-inch (4 cm) double-sided satin—it makes a large, showy flower.

Cut a piece of practice ribbon about 16 inches (40.5 cm) long. Fold one end over three or four times, to make a roll. Sew the roll together at one end, using a sewing needle and thread. Fold the top of the ribbon over and away from you. Roll the sewn roll to the left, toward the folded ribbon, going about halfway around the roll. Sew the bottom fold in place. Turn the ribbon back and down, as before, and roll the ribbon bud to the left, onto the folded length. Stitch bottom. Repeat until rose is the desired size. To finish, cut ribbon at an angle, tuck in the corner, and stitch to base.

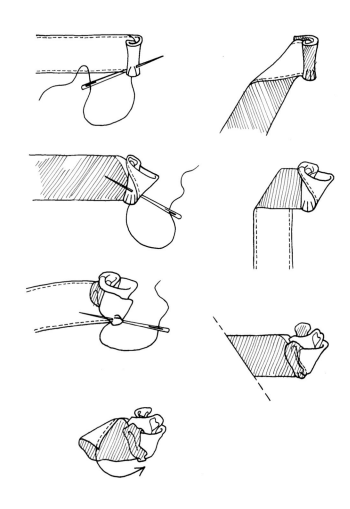

CONCERTINA ROSE

This handsome flower is known by several names (folded rose, for example), but "concertina" is both elegant and apt. Think of the small, accordion-like instrument.

To make this rose, thread a small needle with thread or floss the same color as the ribbon. Knot and set aside.

Now cut a piece of ribbon about 8 inches (20.5 cm) long. Fold it at the center into an L, finger-pressing the crease (1). Fold the horizontal piece backward and to the left (2). Fold the vertical piece to the back and down (3). Fold the horizontal piece to the back and right (4). Continue folding to the back, alternating sections of the ribbon, until all of it is folded. Hold the last fold securely with one hand, allowing the accordioned section to relax. Pull the other end of the ribbon through the folds (5). Using the needle and matching thread, go up through the center of the rose and back down again (6). Position the rose on the fabric; sew down through the fabric, back up through the rose, and back down through both rose and fabric. Knot the thread on the back.

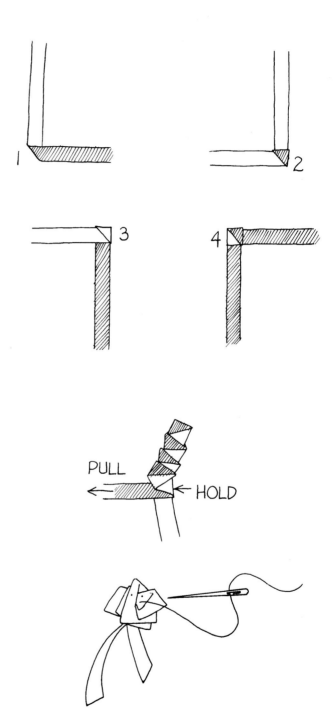

GATHERED ROSE

This is one of the showiest and most three-dimensional flowers. You can vary its size at will—the longer and wider the ribbon, the larger the flower—but to start, cut a piece of 4 mm or 7 mm ribbon about 6 inches (15 cm) long. Also thread a needle with embroidery floss in a matching color.

Fold under one end of the ribbon. With the floss, make running stitches along one long ribbon edge for about 1 inch (2.5 cm). Gather the ribbon and tack it to the background fabric with the floss. Gather another inch of ribbon in the same way and spiral it around the outside. Continue until all the ribbon is gathered and tacked or until the rose is as large as desired. Tuck the raw end under the gathers and tack in place.

To make a two-colored flower, lay a 4 mm ribbon atop a 7 mm ribbon, aligning them along one long edge. Sew ribbons together with a running stitch, then gather as before.

SPIDER WEB ROSE

This woven rose uses much the same technique as your friendly neighborhood arachnid.

Form the spokes of the web with perle cotton or embroidery floss. Come up at 1 and go down at 2—don't pull the thread tight. Come up at 3, taking the needle over the loose thread, and go down at 4. Now add a bar of equal length on each side to complete the base for weaving.

With the ribbon, come up in the center of the web. Moving counter-clockwise, weave the ribbon over and under the spokes, keeping it loose and allowing it to twist. Continue until the spokes are covered.

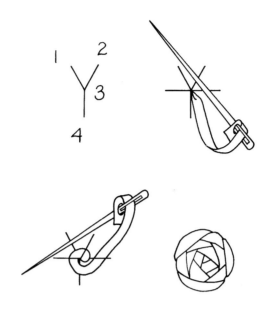

STEM STITCH ROSE

For the center, make a loose French knot. Around the knot, make short, loose stem stitches in concentric circles, working clockwise.

Rosebuds

There are various ways to make rosebuds; here are two of the best.

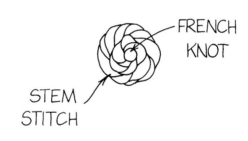

STRAIGHT STITCH

Make three straight stitches, slanting them so they meet at the bottom. Make all three the same color, or use a different color for the center stitch.

LAZY DAISY

Use a lazy daisy stitch for the rosebud; work a fly stitch underneath it for the calyx. (A ribbon bud and a floss calyx work well.)

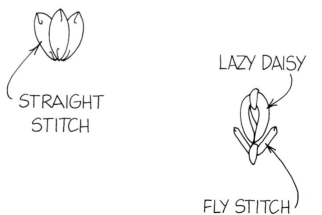

Wildlife

Since every garden has its bugs, you may want to add a few to your silk ribbon version. The bugs below appear on the cover.

Bee

Make the body from a straight stitch and the wings from two straight stitches, using yellow 4 mm ribbon. Using black floss, couch across the body three times and make a French knot head. For a top view, simply add wings on both sides of the body.

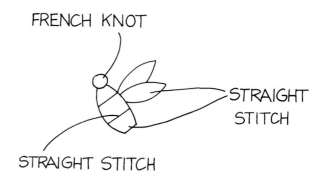

Ladybug

Make a straight stitch body, using red 4 mm ribbon. In black floss, make small French knots for the spots and a larger one for the head. Use pistil stitches for the antennae and a straight stitch to divide the back.

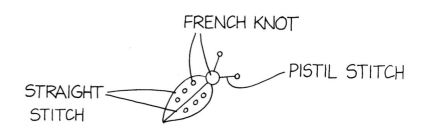

Generic Flying Insect

Make two twisted straight stitches, angling them in a V shape and using 4 mm ribbon. Using black floss, run a straight stitch up the center of the V. With the same floss, anchor the ribbons with French knots, make a French knot head, and add pistil stitch antennae.

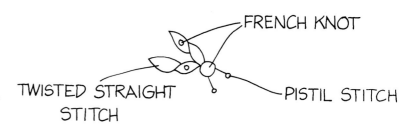

Read On

If you want more suggestions for making ribbon posies, you can't do better than *An Encyclopedia of Ribbon Embroidery Flowers* by Deanna Hall West (San Marcos, CA: ASN Publishing)—a fine little 60-page paperback that details every flower you've ever picked, and many you haven't.

Stitch Icons

⎯⎯	BACKSTITCH		LOOP STITCH
	BULLION KNOT STITCH		LOOP FLOWER
	BUTTONHOLE STITCH		MONTANO KNOW
	CHAIN STITCH		PISTIL STITCH
	COLONIAL KNOT		PLUME STITCH
	COUCHING		STAR STITCH
	CRETAN STITCH		STEM STITCH
	FEATHER STITCH		STRAIGHT STITCH
	FERN STITCH		PADDED STRAIGHT STITCH
	FLY STITCH		TWISTED STRAIGHT STITCH
	FRENCH KNOT		WAVE STITCH
	HERRINGBONE STITCH		WHIPPED RUNNING STITCH
	JAPANESE RIBNBON STITCH		WRAPPED BAR
	TWISTED RIBBON STITCH		BRADFORD ROSE
	LAZY DAISY		CABBAGE ROSE
	BULLION-TIPPED LAZY		CONCERTINA ROSE
	DECORATED LAZY DAISY		GATHERED ROSE
	LEAF STITCH		SPIDER WEB ROSE
			STEM STITCH ROSE

Vest With Fuchsias

Designer: Joan Toomey

YOU WILL NEED

VEST
4 MM AND 7 MM SILK RIBBON
SILK EMBROIDERY FLOSS
CHENILLE NEEDLES
EMBROIDERY NEEDLES

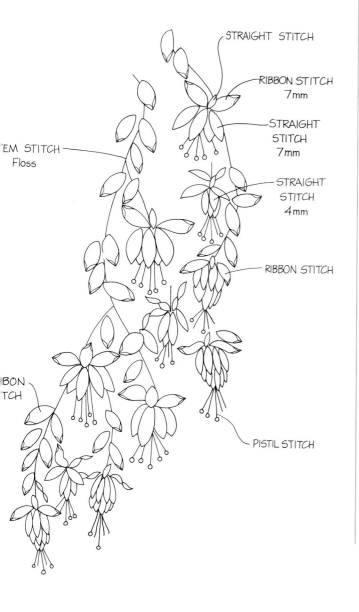

STRAIGHT STITCH

RIBBON STITCH
7mm

STRAIGHT
STITCH
7mm

STRAIGHT
STITCH
4mm

RIBBON STITCH

PISTIL STITCH

STEM STITCH
Floss

BON
TCH

*S*TARTING ABOUT 2 INCHES (5 cm) down from the shoulder seam, work the first stem in stem stitch, using embroidery floss. Work a large pink fuchsia. Work the remaining pink fuchsias, then fill in with other fuchsias. Finally, fill in with the remaining stems (all in stem stitch and embroidery floss) and the leaves. Embroider the opposite side of the vest, changing the flower arrangements somewhat.

Plump pink fuchsias. Work from the center of the flower out, using 7 mm ribbon. For the "skirt," make five straight stitches, spreading the ribbon at the bottom for a full appearance. For the top, work two Japanese ribbon stitches at "rabbit ear" angles, then take a short, straight stitch over the center of them. Add pistil stitches at the bottom in embroidery floss.

Purple fuchsias. Work these in the same way as the pink flowers, with one exception: add a second layer of five petals above the first, overlapping the layers.

Blue and red fuchsias. Using 4 mm ribbon and working from the center out, take three straight stitches for the body of the flower. Change color and work four Japanese ribbon stitches or twisted ribbon stitches at the top. Add pistil stitches at the bottom.

Hot Pink Bomber Jacket

Designer: Sara Spiece

YOU WILL NEED

PURCHASED JACKET
4 MM, 7 MM, AND 13 MM SILK RIBBON
CHENILLE NEEDLES
EMBROIDERY NEEDLES

MENTALLY DIVIDE THE JACKET into vertical sections. Starting from the top down, work the top third or fourth of the jacket, then the next third, and so on.

Work the vertical lines of feather stitch in perle cotton, to help provide a visual framework for the flowers. Then add flowers at will, positioning the larger ones first if you like, but otherwise working pretty much as the ribbon moves you. Several stitches predominate on this pattern: loop stitches for buds and flowers, Japanese ribbon stitches for flowers and leaves, lazy daisy stitches, and an abundance of knots both singly and in clusters. A few large flowers are scattered about: spider web, concertina, and folded roses and a large plume-stitch posy near the bottom.

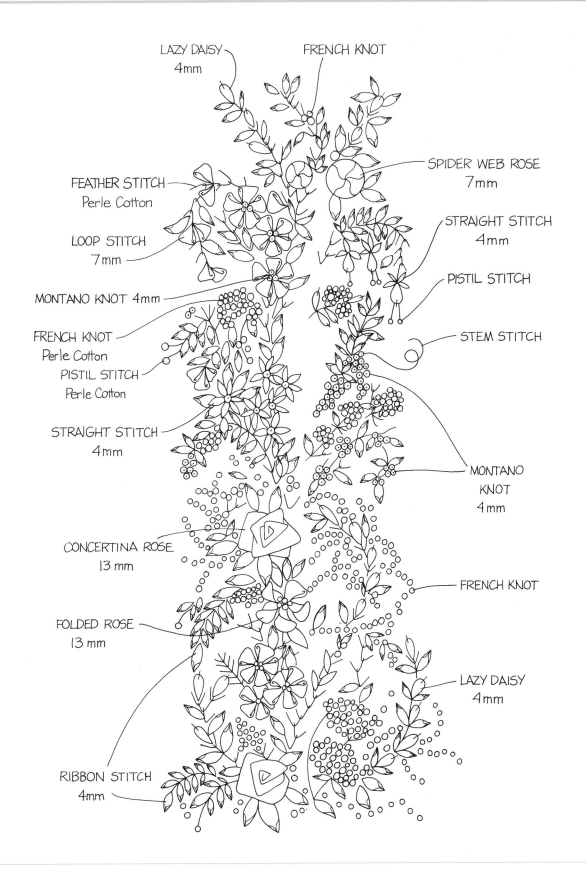

LAZY DAISY
4mm

FRENCH KNOT

SPIDER WEB ROSE
7mm

FEATHER STITCH
Perle Cotton

STRAIGHT STITCH
4mm

LOOP STITCH
7mm

PISTIL STITCH

MONTANO KNOT 4mm

STEM STITCH

FRENCH KNOT
Perle Cotton

PISTIL STITCH
Perle Cotton

STRAIGHT STITCH
4mm

MONTANO
KNOT
4mm

CONCERTINA ROSE
13 mm

FRENCH KNOT

FOLDED ROSE
13 mm

LAZY DAISY
4mm

RIBBON STITCH
4mm

Silk Ribbon Jewelry

Designer: Annie Coan

YOU WILL NEED

FOR THE JEWELRY

BUTTON MOLDS 1⅝ OR 2 INCHES IN DIAMETER (4.1 OR 5 CM), AVAILABLE IN FABRIC STORES

3-INCH (7.5 CM) SQUARE PIECES OF FABRIC OR ENOUGH TO COVER THE MOLD

SYNTHETIC SUEDE

CRAFT GLUE

PIN BACKS FOR THE PINS

JUMP RINGS AND DECORATIVE CORD FOR THE PENDANTS

FOR THE EMBROIDERY

2 MM, 4 MM, AND 7 MM SILK RIBBON

METALLIC THREAD

BEADS

CHENILLE NEEDLES

EMBROIDERY NEEDLES

BEADING NEEDLE OR OTHER SMALL-EYED NEEDLE

MAKING JEWELRY EMBROI-DERED with silk ribbon is so quick and easy that you'll want to try out a number of items and a variety of styles to go with just about any outfit you own.

Annie Coan believes that spontaneous ribbon embroidery can produce fine and satisfying results—not following a pattern, but taking needle and ribbon in hand and following where they lead. Fabric jewelry is the perfect place to try it out.

Pat Moore enjoys adapting traditional stitches to a small canvas—spider web roses, lazy daisy flowers, wisteria that consists of groups of French knots, and stem stitch leaves and stems. She's especially fond of beads,

both as flower centers and as background fillers.

To begin, cover a button mold by stretching the fabric around the front of the mold and hooking it into the teeth in back. Be careful not to stretch the fabric too tight, as you will want to leave room for stitching. When the fabric is secure, snap the back of the mold into place.

Now work the embroidery. To create a freeform design, use your imagination (and chenille needles) to stitch at will, blending and contrasting the silk ribbon with the color and texture of the background fabric. Coan tends to use simple stitches, such as straight stitches, Japanese ribbon stitches, and lazy daisy stitches in metallic thread. For a more traditional approach, begin by positioning a few large posies. If desired, add stems and leaves.

Designer: Pat Moore

Use the beading needle to sew on colored beads with metallic thread. You can cluster small beads at the center of a silk flower or randomly distribute a variety of beads throughout the design. Beads suspended from the jewelry on heavy thread also create a nice effect.

To finish a pendant, glue a piece of felt or synthetic suede over the back. Hand-stitch a jump ring to the top of the fabric and thread a piece of satin cording through the ring.

To finish a pin, glue the pin back mechanism to the back of the button mold. Cut out a piece of felt or synthetic suede to fit the back of the mold. Make holes in the suede to fit over the projecting ends of the pin back. Open the pin, fit the suede down over it, and glue in place.

Velvet Cap

Designer: Pat Moore

*D*ESIGNER *PAT MOORE* relied exclusively on ribbon to create this jazzy cap. Starting at the center, she first worked the larger flowers. Petals range from lazy daisy stitches to Japanese ribbon stitches, from stacked loops to gathered roses. Then she added stems in 4 mm ribbon—some in stem stitch, others in backstitch. Finally, she filled in with French knots up and down the stems.

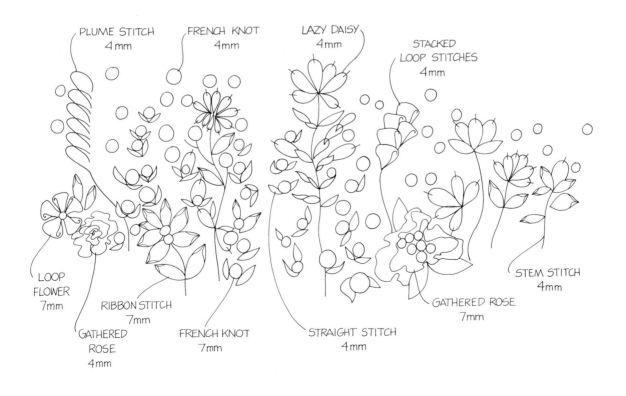

Embroidered Denim Vest

Designer: Sara Spiece

A FORGETTABLE DENIM VEST BECOMES A MEMORABLE PART of the wardrobe when embellished with silk ribbon. Starting at a shoulder seam, work down each side. Work the vines in stem stitch first, to help you position the flowers and leaves. Then embroider the flowers: decorated lazy daisies, Japanese ribbon stitches, straight stitches, and clusters of Montano knots. Add extra decorative greenery in fern stitch, using embroidery floss.

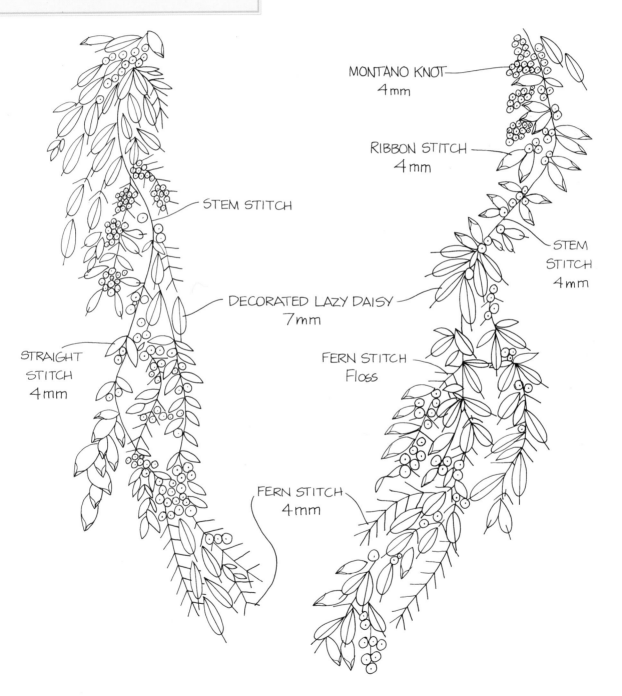

YOU WILL NEED
VEST (PURCHASED OR HOMEMADE)
4 MM AND 7 MM SILK RIBBON
EMBROIDERY FLOSS
CHENILLE NEEDLE
EMBROIDERY NEEDLES

MONTANO KNOT
4mm

RIBBON STITCH
4mm

STEM STITCH

STEM
STITCH
4mm

DECORATED LAZY DAISY
7mm

STRAIGHT
STITCH
4mm

FERN STITCH
Floss

FERN STITCH
4mm

Embroidered Bowler

Designer: Ruth Harris

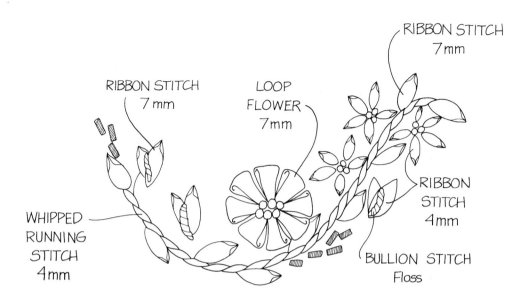

RIBBON STITCH
7mm

RIBBON STITCH
7mm

LOOP
FLOWER
7mm

RIBBON
STITCH
4mm

WHIPPED
RUNNING
STITCH
4mm

BULLION STITCH
Floss

YOU WILL NEED

PURCHASED HAT

4 MM AND 7 MM SILK RIBBON

SILK BUTTONHOLE TWIST

CHENILLE NEEDLES

EMBROIDERY NEEDLES

SEED BEADS AND BUGLE BEADS

MATCHING SEWING THREAD

*F*IRST MARK THE SHAPE and location of the long, curved stem, using a running stitch in silk buttonhole twist. Then work over this line in 4 mm ribbon with a whipped running stitch. Work the large loop flower, using seed beads for the center. Next work the anthuriums, using two leaf stitches in 7 mm ribbon for the petals and a bullion stitch in buttonhole twist for the centers. Add the remaining flowers, each worked with five Japanese ribbon stitch petals and a bead center. Add leaves of Japanese ribbon stitch and finish with two sprays of bugle beads.

Embroidered Necktie

Designer: Patricia Clark

YOU WILL NEED

PURCHASED NECKTIE
4 MM AND 7 MM RIBBON
PERLE COTTON
SEWING THREAD TO MATCH TIE
CHENILLE NEEDLES
EMBROIDERY NEEDLES

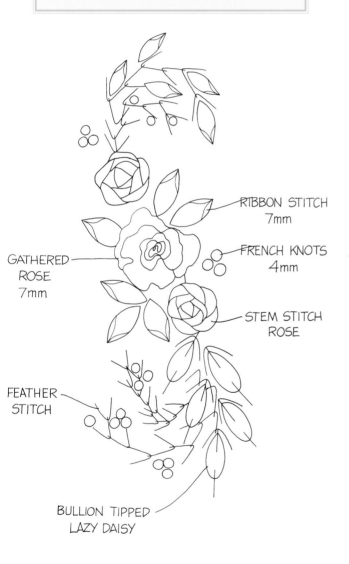

RIBBON STITCH
7mm

FRENCH KNOTS
4mm

GATHERED
ROSE
7mm

STEM STITCH
ROSE

FEATHER
STITCH

BULLION TIPPED
LAZY DAISY

*S*NIP THE STITCHES that hold the back of the tie closed, clipping up about 14 inches (35.5 cm) from the bottom. Open the back and remove the clipped threads. Inside will probably be an unattached interfacing. Baste it to the front of the tie, sewing along the edges. Trace the overall S shape of the pattern lightly onto the front of the tie, positioning the center of the design about 8 inches (20.5 cm) from the pointed bottom.

Using the perle cotton, work feather stitch along the S-shaped line, beginning at each end and working toward the center. Then work the roses: a large gathered rose in 7 mm ribbon, and two stem stitch roses in 4 mm ribbon. Add five rosebuds at the bottom of the design in long-tipped lazy daisies, using 4 mm ribbon for each one. Using 7 mm ribbon, work leaves in Japanese ribbon stitch. At the top of the design, add a spray of red buds in 4 mm ribbon with Japanese ribbon stitch. Finish off with strategically placed French knots in 4 mm ribbon.

Press the tie around the embroidery, if necessary. Remove the basting thread and slipstitch the tie closed.

Hair Ribbon

Designer: Ruth Harris

*F*IRST WORK THE SPIDER WEB rose in the center of the design, using a color that complements the hair ribbon. Then add a few rosebuds, some in straight stitch, some in lazy daisy, working the calyxes in fly stitch in silk buttonhole twist. Add ribbon French knots and finish with stem stitch stems in buttonhole twist.

Although the hair ribbon shown has a design on only one side, feel free to work a matching or quite different collection of flowers on the other end of the bow.

If ready-made hair ribbons are not available in your choice of colors, it's easy to make your own. Simply cut a piece of wide grosgrain ribbon about 16 inches (40.5 cm) long and hem the long edges. Fold each end of the

ribbon toward the center, to produce a thick, multi-layer bow. Stitch the bow together at the center. Cut a narrow strip of grosgrain ribbon and wrap it around the center. Tack the ends of the narrow strip to the inside of the bow. Glue the finished ribbon to a barrette back, available in most craft stores and wherever jewelry-making supplies are sold.

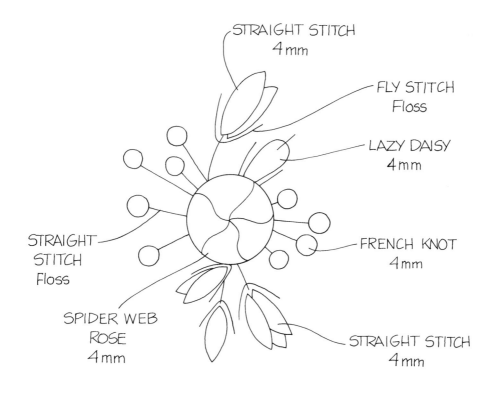

STRAIGHT STITCH
4mm

FLY STITCH
Floss

LAZY DAISY
4mm

FRENCH KNOT
4mm

STRAIGHT STITCH
4mm

STRAIGHT STITCH
Floss

SPIDER WEB ROSE
4mm

Embroidered Blouse

Designer: Pat Moore

A ROW OF EMBROIDERY around the neckline can turn a simple blouse into a special garment. Starting in the center of the front, work ribbon flowers, varying the stitches as well as the colors and sizes of the ribbon to suit yourself. Shown are spider web roses, loop flowers, French knot grapes, and lazy daisy daisies. Next add ribbon leaves, working some in straight stitch, some in Japanese ribbon stitch, and some in lazy daisy if you need extra fullness. Finally, connect the flowers with a stem stitch vine worked in silk buttonhole twist.

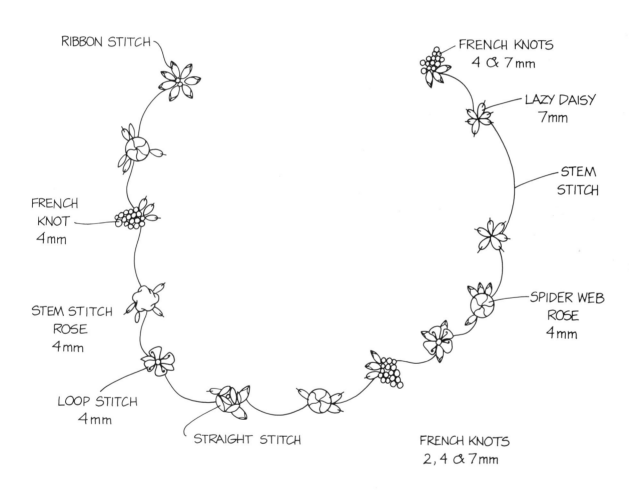

RIBBON STITCH

FRENCH KNOTS
4 & 7mm

LAZY DAISY
7mm

STEM
STITCH

FRENCH
KNOT
4mm

STEM STITCH
ROSE
4mm

SPIDER WEB
ROSE
4mm

LOOP STITCH
4mm

STRAIGHT STITCH

FRENCH KNOTS
2, 4 & 7mm

Ribboned Beret

Designer: Anne Felden

*F*OR THIS ENDEAR-
ING BERET, Anne
Felden used hand-
dyed, bias-cut silk ribbon for the
central, three-dimensional flower.
This large, soft bloom shows off
the virtues of bias-cut ribbon particularly well. This ribbon is made
by cutting silk fabric at a 45-
degree angle to the weave. Because
it's cut on the bias, the ribbon
won't ravel and its edges can be
left unsealed—which makes it
extremely soft and allows it to
drape very well indeed.

Bias-cut ribbon will fray, on
the other hand, especially if pulled
repeatedly through a very tightly
woven fabric. Some designers like
the frayed appearance, because it
gives a nice "period" look. To
avoid fraying, use a large-eyed chenille needle and work with short
lengths of ribbon.

Figure 1

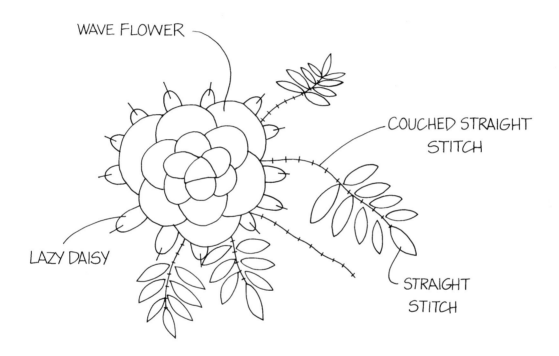

WAVE FLOWER

COUCHED STRAIGHT STITCH

LAZY DAISY

STRAIGHT STITCH

To make a similar hat, start with the large flower, which is a giant wave stitch. First make the base of the flower in buttonhole stitch with embroidery floss. Then, using the ⅜-inch ribbon, work lazy daisy stitches around the outside of the base, placing a stitch in every other segment (see Fig. 1). Now continue with the wave stitch, weaving the ⅝-inch (1.6 cm) silk ribbon in and out of the base. Then make the leaves, couching the stems with rayon thread and working the leaves in straight stitches of ⅜-inch (1 cm) ribbon.

Flower Garden Vest

Designer: Cathie Bates

SING A CHALK PENCIL (if your vest is dark), draw a line down the vest, indicating where the center of your design will be. In doing the embroidery, designer Cathie Bates started at the white calla lilies on the right-hand curve and worked her way up, then down, from there.

From the top down are foxglove (French knots at top, petals in Japanese ribbon stitch, leaves in straight stitch); bleeding hearts (straight stitch petals, pistil stitch centers); impatiens (petals and leaves in straight stitch); a rose bush (buds are Japanese ribbon stitch, large roses are loop stitch with French knot centers); tulips (lazy daisy petals, straight stitch leaves); snapdragons (French knot and straight stitch petals, straight stitch leaves); snow drops (straight stitch); calla lilies (wrapped bar centers, lazy daisy petals, ribbon stitch leaves); violets (straight stitch petals with French knot centers); crocus (straight stitch); hyacinths (French and colonial knots); more tulips; wind flowers (straight stitch); and geraniums (colonial knots). Stems are in stem stitch. For bees and ladybugs, see page 28.

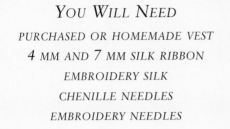

YOU WILL NEED

PURCHASED OR HOMEMADE VEST
4 MM AND 7 MM SILK RIBBON
EMBROIDERY SILK
CHENILLE NEEDLES
EMBROIDERY NEEDLES

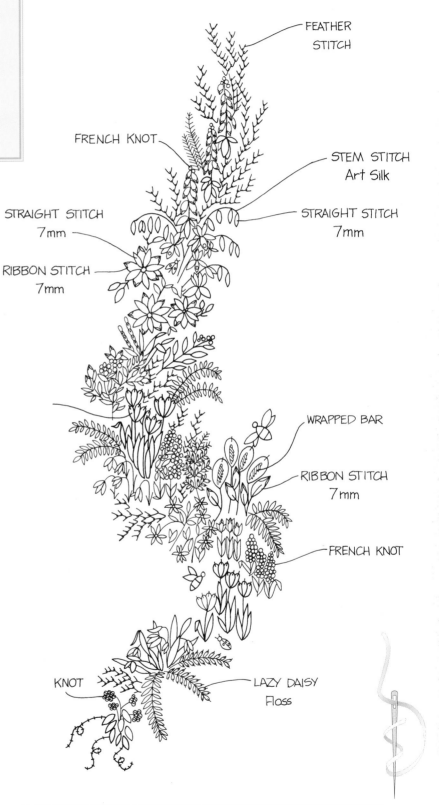

FEATHER
STITCH

FRENCH KNOT

STEM STITCH
Art Silk

STRAIGHT STITCH
7mm

STRAIGHT STITCH
7mm

RIBBON STITCH
7mm

WRAPPED BAR

RIBBON STITCH
7mm

FRENCH KNOT

KNOT

LAZY DAISY
Floss

Embellished Handbag

Designer: Katheryn Foutz

YOU WILL NEED

¼ YARD *(32 CM) HEAVY COTTON FABRIC, SUCH AS BROCADE UPHOLSTERY FABRIC*

¼ YARD *SHEER GOLD METALLIC FABRIC*

¼ YARD *FLEECE PADDING*

¼ YARD *TAFFETA FOR PURSE LINING*

1 YARD *(92 CM) THIN BLACK/GOLD METALLIC CORDING*

BLACK/GOLD METALLIC FLOSS

4 MM *AND* 7 MM *SILK RIBBON*

BUGLE BEADS AND TINY SEED BEADS

1 YARD OF ¾-INCH *(2 CM) WIRE-EDGED RIBBON FOR ROSE AND BUDS*

6-INCH *(15 CM) LENGTH OF* ¾-INCH *(2 CM) FLAT LACE*

¾ YARD *(68 CM) BLACK/GOLD LACE TRIM* ⅜ INCH *(1 CM) WIDE*

DECORATIVE BUTTONS

7 X 7-INCH *(18 X 18 CM) PIECE OF VINTAGE LACE*

1½ YARDS *(137 CM) DECORATIVE CORDING, FOR TRIM AND STRAP*

4-INCH *(10 CM) TASSEL*

FABRIC MARKER

CHENILLE NEEDLES, BEADING NEEDLE

*I*N ADDITION TO STANDARD silk ribbon embroidery, this elegant bag has two large rosebuds and one central rose made from wire-edged ribbon. Both are folded by hand and then tacked onto the purse.

Using back/flap pattern A, cut one piece of cotton fabric, one sheer gold metallic fabric, one taffeta lining, and one fleece. Also cut one piece from each fabric using front pattern B.

To construct the purse, start with the back/flap section. Place the sheer gold metallic fabric over the cotton fabric, and the cotton fabric over the fleece. Secure with pins and hand or machine baste together around the edges. Repeat this process for front section. Do not sew in lining at this time, as the embroidery and most of the embellishments will be completed before the purse is lined and assembled.

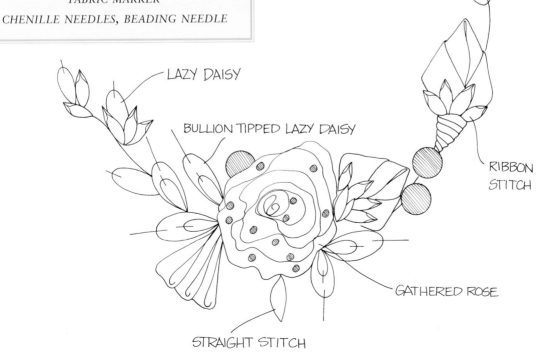

LAZY DAISY

BULLION TIPPED LAZY DAISY

RIBBON STITCH

GATHERED ROSE

STRAIGHT STITCH

Transfer design to right side of purse flap. To begin the embroidery, first arrange the thin metallic cording on flap and secure with pins. Hand-tack cording in place with gold metallic floss, removing the pins as you stitch.

Using 7 mm ribbon, make bullion-tipped lazy daisy stitches for the leaves and the small buds. Using 4 mm ribbon, make smaller lazy daisy stitches over the leaves to highlight them. Further accent each leaf with a loop of bugle beads stitched in the center. Make small Japanese ribbon stitches at the base of each bud.

Next, make the two large buds from wire-edged ribbon. For each bud, cut a piece of wire-edged ribbon and a piece of flat lace, each about 2 inches (5 cm) long. Find the center of the ribbon and fold one side, then the other side, over and down, to make a point.

Fold the lace around the base of the ribbon. Gather or twist all four ends together and wrap with thread or fine wire at the base of the bud to secure it (see Fig. 1). Lay the buds on the purse and tack them in place. Using 4 mm ribbon, cover the twisted "stem" of each bud with straight stitches, then make four Japanese ribbon stitches around the base.

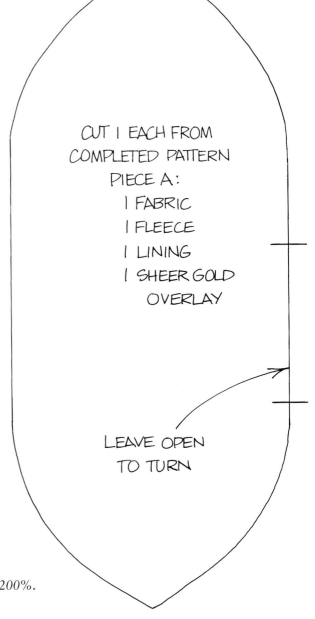

CUT 1 EACH FROM
COMPLETED PATTERN
PIECE A:
   1 FABRIC
   1 FLEECE
   1 LINING
   1 SHEER GOLD
      OVERLAY

LEAVE OPEN
TO TURN

PURSE FRONT B
CUT 1 EACH:
   1 FABRIC
   1 FLEECE
   1 LINING
   1 SHEER GOLD
      OVERLAY

LEAVE OPEN
TO TURN

Photocopy at 200%.

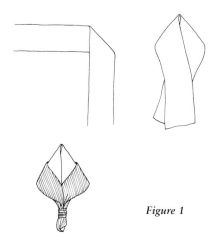

Figure 1

To make the large, central rose of wire-edged ribbon, tie a knot 1 inch (2.5 cm) from one end of the remaining length of ribbon, forming a stem. Now move to the other end of the ribbon. On one long edge, carefully push the ribbon fabric along the wire toward the knot; the wire will become exposed as the ribbon gathers along it. Holding the wire, continue to push the ribbon along the wire toward the knot, gathering the ribbon tightly. Wind the gathered edge of the ribbon around the stem just below the knot. Fold the cut end of the ribbon down and out of sight so that the raw edges are not visible. Wrap the wire tightly around the stem below the gathers. Trim the wire and the stem below the wrapped wire (see Fig. 2).

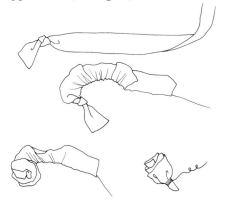

Figure 2

Roll and smash the rose between the palms of your hands to give it a crinkly, vintage look. Arrange it in place on your design and tack it down with tiny seed beads. Finish the rose by adding three loops of beads in the center. Make three 1⅓-inch (3.3 cm) loops of the black/gold lace trim, tuck them to the side of the rose, and tack them down. Hand-stitch buttons on flap as desired.

Place the piece of vintage lace over the purse front and hand-stitch to secure.

ASSEMBLY

Place the back/flap and its taffeta lining piece right sides together. Machine stitch ¼ inch (.5 cm) around the outside edge, leaving open where indicated. Clip curves, turn right side out, and press edges. Fold edges of opening under and hand-stitch closed. Repeat for purse front.

Place purse front over purse back/flap with lined sides together and bottom points matching. Whipstitch sides together with strong thread.

Lay one end of the cording at the bottom point of the purse.

Using gold thread, whipstitch the cording along one outside edge of the purse, continuing up to the junction of the front and back. Then leave a section of the cording unattached to act as a strap, making it as long as you like. Then whipstitch the cording to the other side of the purse, starting at junction of front and back and working down to the point. Trim any excess cording ends. Tack the tassel at the point, to cover the raw ends of cording. Stitch a couple of decorative buttons at the top of the tassel.

To finish the purse, hand-stitch the length of black/gold lace around the front flap.

Moderately Crazy Patch Vest

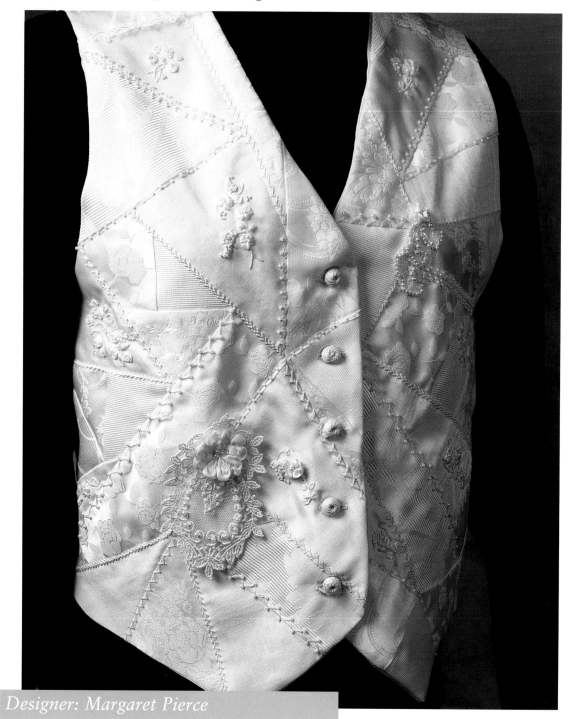

Designer: Margaret Pierce

You Will Need

VEST PATTERN

*SCRAPS (PATCHES) OF FABRIC IN
VARIOUS SHAPES*

MUSLIN (FOR THE FOUNDATION)

4 MM AND 7 MM SILK RIBBON

SILK EMBROIDERY THREAD

CHENILLE NEEDLES

EMBROIDERY NEEDLES

CRAZY PATCH OFTEN INVOLVES A riot of wildly different colors, but designer Margaret Pierce chose to limit her palette to shades of white and cream, allowing fabric textures and patterns to provide interest and variety.

THE CRAZY PATCH

To make a similar vest, cut a left front, a right front, and a back from muslin, using the pattern pieces for the vest. These muslin pieces will form the foundation of your crazy patching. (Note: Your vest pattern may have more or fewer pieces that will be visible in the finished vest. Whatever you have, cut them from muslin.)

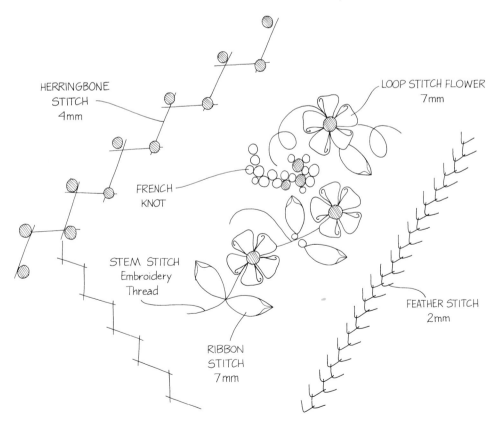

HERRINGBONE
STITCH
4mm

LOOP STITCH FLOWER
7mm

FRENCH
KNOT

STEM STITCH
Embroidery
Thread

FEATHER STITCH
2mm

RIBBON
STITCH
7mm

Lay a patch on one of the muslin foundation pieces and pin it in place. Lay a second patch on the first one, right sides together. Using a ¼-inch (.5 cm) seam allowance, machine stitch the two patches together, leaving ¼ inch unsewn at both ends of the seam. Turn the second patch up, press the seam, and pin. See Figure 1. Continue adding patches in this way until the entire piece of muslin is covered. If odd areas cannot be machine stitched, turn under ¼-inch seam allowance and whip-stitch the patch in place by hand. Repeat for remaining vest pieces.

Turn the patched pieces over and trim around the outside edges, following the muslin foundation, so that the muslin and the patches are flush.

THE EMBROIDERY

Work the ribbon embroidery on the right side of the vest pieces. Work embroidery stitches over some of the quilted seam lines: feather stitch and herringbone stitch work especially well, but a flat piece of lace or a ribbon simply tacked down with beads is also attractive. To dress up the stitching even more, sew seed beads into the Vs of the herringbone stitches.

Work flowers at various places on the vest. A large loop flower with leaves of Japanese ribbon stitch is dramatic when worked in 7 mm ribbon. Make clusters of wisteria in 4 mm ribbon, using French knots for the blooms and ribbon stitch for the leaves.

FINISHING

Treating the crazy patch pieces as normal pieces of fabric (although they are in fact much more interesting), sew the vest together, following the pattern instructions.

Figure 1

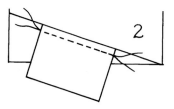

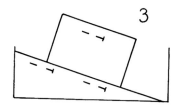

Embroidered Locket

Designer: Anne Felden

To turn a broken old wristwatch into a necklace, first remove the watchband, the back of the case, and the works. Then trace around the case on the linen and work the embroidery in the traced area. Stitch the embroidered linen to the interfacing, cut out, and insert into frame. Glue pieces of suede to the back of the linen to secure.

To make the tassel, cut 12 pieces of heavy thread double the length of the tassel and tie each thread to the case, leaving equal tails. Thread the beading needle onto a tail and string on 12 seed beads; then take the needle through the large accent bead. Repeat with each tail. Now string seed beads onto a tail and, skipping the last bead, needle back up the row. Tie off between two beads. Repeat with remaining tails.

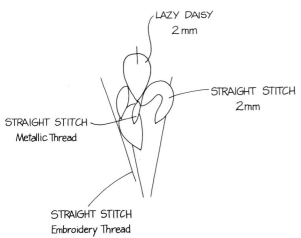

LAZY DAISY
2 mm

STRAIGHT STITCH
2mm

STRAIGHT STITCH
Metallic Thread

STRAIGHT STITCH
Embroidery Thread

Beribboned Hat

Designer: Ruth Harris

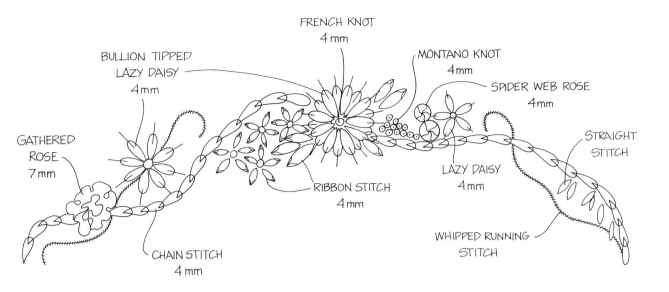

FRENCH KNOT
4 mm

BULLION TIPPED
LAZY DAISY
4mm

MONTANO KNOT
4mm

SPIDER WEB ROSE
4mm

GATHERED
ROSE
7 mm

STRAIGHT
STITCH

RIBBON STITCH
4 mm

LAZY DAISY
4mm

CHAIN STITCH
4 mm

WHIPPED RUNNING
STITCH

YOU WILL NEED

PURCHASED FABRIC HAT WITH FLAP

4 MM SILK RIBBON

4 MM AND 7 MM ORGANDY RIBBON

*DECORATIVE THREAD, BUTTONS,
SEED BEADS*

*SEWING NEEDLE AND THREAD
TO MATCH BEADS*

CHENILLE NEEDLES

EMBROIDERY NEEDLES

ORGANDY RIBBON FLOWERS add exuberant touches to this charming hat. Work the pattern twice to encircle the hat. Begin with the chain stitch vine, then add the shasta daisies in 4 mm ribbon. To make the daisies, work two concentric circles of straight stitches, with the inner row covering the spaces between the stitches in the outer row. Then fill the centers with French knots.

Now work the gathered roses with organdy ribbon. Embroider the bullion-tipped lazy daisy flowers, then the plain lazy daisy stitches. Add tendrils in whipped running stitch with decorative thread. Next work the spider web roses, Montano knots, Japanese ribbon stitch flowers with French knot centers, and ribbon stitch leaves. Add seed beads to the center of the organdy roses. If there's a bothersome empty spot, add a decorative button.

Three-Flower Brooch

Designer: Stephanie Williams

$\mathcal{M}$AKING THE ROSE. Cut five petals from 32 mm silk ribbon, using the pattern shown (see Fig. 1). Turn down the top edge of each petal and run a gathering stitch along it (see Fig. 2). Pull gathers tight and knot thread. Turn under the raw ends and slip-stitch the sides together. Run a gathering

YOU WILL NEED

32 MM PINK SILK RIBBON FOR THE WILD ROSE

7 MM LILAC SILK RIBBON FOR THE LILAC

13 MM WHITE SILK RIBBON FOR THE CARNATION

32 MM GREEN RIBBON FOR THE LEAF

SILK THREAD

PIECE OF STIFF INTERFACING ABOUT 5 X 5 INCHES (12.5 X 12.5 CM)

FELT

PIN BACK

GLUE

THIN SILK NEEDLE

INVISIBLE THREAD

stitch across the bottom of the petal and gather (see Fig. 3).

Figure 1

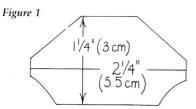

Arrange the petals in a circle on the interfacing, leaving a small hole in the middle for the center of the flower. Sew the petals to the interfacing at their gathered ends.

To make the center of the rose, cut a thin cardboard circle about ¼ inch (.5 cm) in diameter. Place a piece of silk fabric in a small embroidery hoop and trace the cardboard circle on the fabric. Using a single strand of silk thread, fill the whole circle with French knots. Run a gathering stitch around the circle of

Figure 2

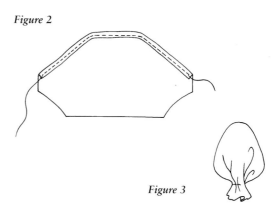

Figure 3

knots, cut the fabric close to the stitches, and pull gathers tight around the cardboard. Knot the thread, run a needle through the center of the rose petals, and sew the center into place, tacking along the sides of the rose.

To make the stamens, use the same silk thread as the center. Knot the end of the thread (snip the end, if necessary). Working from front to back, insert the needle at one edge of the center of the flower; pull the needle through until stamen is the right length. Knot in the back. Continue this process all around the center of the rose.

MAKING THE LEAF

Cut a piece of 32 mm ribbon about 3 inches (7.5 cm) long. Fold the ends down and run a gathering stitch as shown in Fig. 4. Pull gathers tight (see Fig. 5). Sew leaf down next to rose with any raw edges hidden under rose petal.

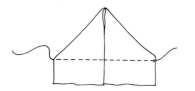

Figure 4   Figure 5

MAKING THE LILAC

Sketch the shape of a lilac bloom on the interfacing. Cut a piece of 7 mm lilac ribbon about 4 inches (10 cm) long. Using a fabric marker, mark dots on the edges of the ribbon, placing them 7 mm apart in a zigzag pattern (see Fig. 6). Use a piece of 7 mm–wide ribbon as a "ruler." Thread a thin silk needle with silk thread, knot it, and run a gathering stitch from dot to dot (see Fig. 6 again); pull tight.

Figure 6

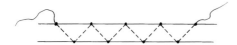

Bring needle through ribbon where the first knot was made, forming a lilac bloom (see Fig 7). Pull tight, knot, and trim raw edges. Run needle and thread through base several times,

Figure 7

pulling tight each time, and shape gathers to look like a lilac. As each bloom is completed, sew it to the interfacing, filling in the lilac shape.

MAKING THE CARNATION

Cut a piece of 13 mm silk ribbon 18 to 24 inches (45.5 to 61 cm) long. Turn one end down to make the center of the flower (see Fig. 8). Run a gathering stitch along the bottom edge of the ribbon. Using invisible thread, run another gathering stitch along the top

Figure 8

edge. Gather both threads gently, starting at the end you turned down. Beginning with the turned end, start rolling ribbon to create the carnation. Using a new piece of thread, tack the bottom of the carnation together as you roll (see Fig. 9). Continue in this manner until carnation is completed. Turn down the last end as you did the first, stitch, and cut remaining ribbon off. Attach carnation to interfacing.

Figure 9

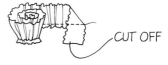

CUT OFF

FINISHING THE BROOCH

Cut out the interfacing close to the design, so that it is not visible from the front. Cut out a piece of poster board and a piece of felt to match the interfacing. Glue poster board to the interfacing. Sew the bar pin to felt, and glue the felt to the poster board.

Bolero Jacket

YOU WILL NEED

JACKET MADE FROM FABRIC THAT
HAS A WOVEN DESIGN (THIS ONE IS
COTTON DAMASK WITH A PAISLEY
DESIGN)

4 MM AND 7 MM SILK RIBBON

SILK EMBROIDERY THREAD

CHENILLE NEEDLES

EMBROIDERY NEEDLES

SEED BEADS

PURCHASED PASSEMENTERIE TASSEL
AND ROSETTE

THREAD TO MATCH BEADS

W HETHER YOU MAKE
THE jacket or buy it,
the embroidery is
determined by the design of the fabric.
Designer Margaret Pierce outlined six of
the large paisley designs by couching
around them with 4 mm ribbon, anchor-
ing the stitches with small beads.

Within the paisley shapes are clusters
of spider web roses with lazy daisy
leaves, both worked in 7 mm ribbon.
Clusters of French knots are embroidered in 4 mm ribbon, and stems are
done in stem stitch and silk embroidery
thread. The tassel and rosette are sewn
onto the jacket, as are clusters of beads
for additional embellishment.

Designer: Margaret Pierce

Velvet Jacket With Roses

Designer: Joan Toomey

*T*HIS LAVISH SPRAY OF ROSES drapes over the shoulder—front, back, and down the side. On the pattern shown, the vertical center falls on top of the shoulder. The roses increase in size as they move from the outside of the design toward the center.

First work the sprays of rosebuds, using padded straight stitch and 4 mm silk ribbon. Next work spider web roses and concertina roses, the outer ones in 4 mm, the inner ones in 7 mm ribbon. Add cabbage roses in 13 mm silk ribbon, then in 1¼-inch (3 cm) satin ribbon. Work the floss stems in stem stitch and fill in with leaves of twisted straight stitch.

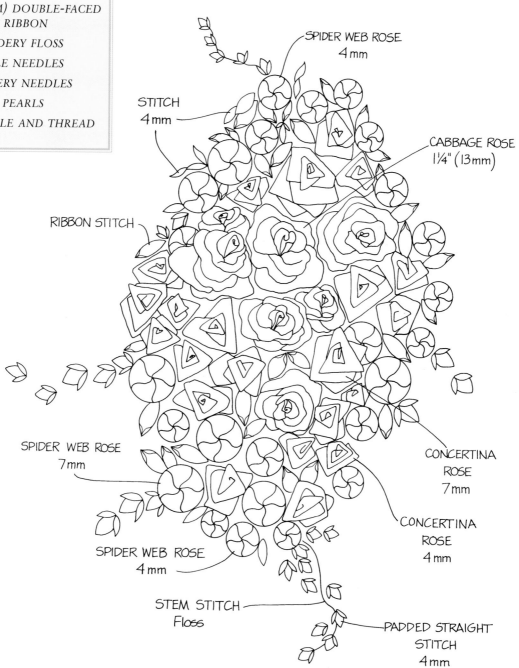

SPIDER WEB ROSE
4mm

STITCH
4mm

CABBAGE ROSE
1¼" (13mm)

RIBBON STITCH

SPIDER WEB ROSE
7mm

SPIDER WEB ROSE
4mm

CONCERTINA
ROSE
7mm

CONCERTINA
ROSE
4mm

STEM STITCH
Floss

PADDED STRAIGHT
STITCH
4mm

Child's Headband

Designer: Ruth Harris

A PURCHASED HEADBAND can be enlivened with an almost random collection of flowers, selected to suit the tastes of the designer and the little girl who will wear it. Start by positioning the larger posies: spider web and concertina roses, decorated and bullion-tipped lazy daisy stitches. Then fill in with the smaller details: Montano knots, straight stitch rosebuds, feather stitches, leaves, and beads. To work the design shown in the pattern, photocopy the pattern, cut out the two illustrations on the photocopy, and lay one illustration on top of the other, matching the vertical lines, to make one long band of flowers.

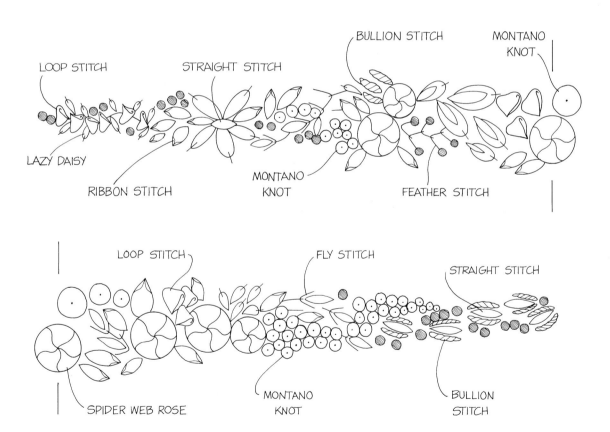

Snazzy Socks

YOU WILL NEED

PAIR OF SOCKS

4 MM SILK RIBBON

CHENILLE NEEDLE

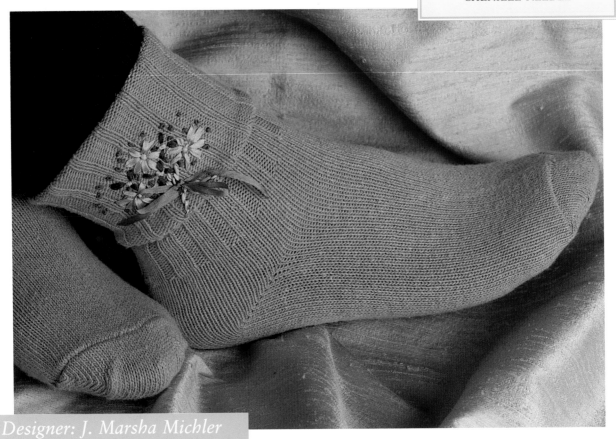

Designer: J. Marsha Michler

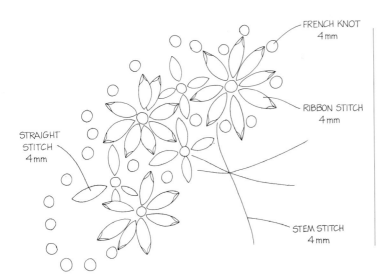

FRENCH KNOT
4mm

RIBBON STITCH
4mm

STRAIGHT
STITCH
4mm

STEM STITCH
4mm

*S*TART BY WORKING THE LARGE flowers, using French knots for the centers and Japanese ribbon stitch for the petals. Then work the "thinner" flowers with French knot centers and straight stitch petals. Add stems in stem stitch and a scattering of French knots around the flowers. Thread the needle with ribbon for the bow and take it under the center of the stems. Remove the needle and tie the ribbon in a bow.

Rose-Covered Sweater

Designer: Pat Moore

A garden's worth of roses is scattered along the front, over the shoulder, and down the back of this sweater. To embroider your own, select ribbons in your favorite rose colors and apply them randomly in a variety of stitches.

Since designer Pat Moore is partial to spider web roses, they predominate on her sweater. She worked most of them with two colors (and often two sizes) of ribbon in the needle at the same time. Bradford roses add their well-pruned look. Several types resemble the old-fashioned single roses of Grandmother's day: Japanese ribbon stitches that spiral out from a center point, loop ribbon roses, and straight stitch flowers. The gathered roses consist of two ribbons worked at the same time. Loose French knots make up the tiny flowers; the leaves are worked in Japanese ribbon stitch.

Garden Sampler

Designer: Cathie Bates

*L*IGHTLY PENCIL A GRID on the fabric and embroider over it in feather stitch, using embroidery floss. Working one square at a time, begin with the flower stem, then stitch the flower, and finish with the leaves.

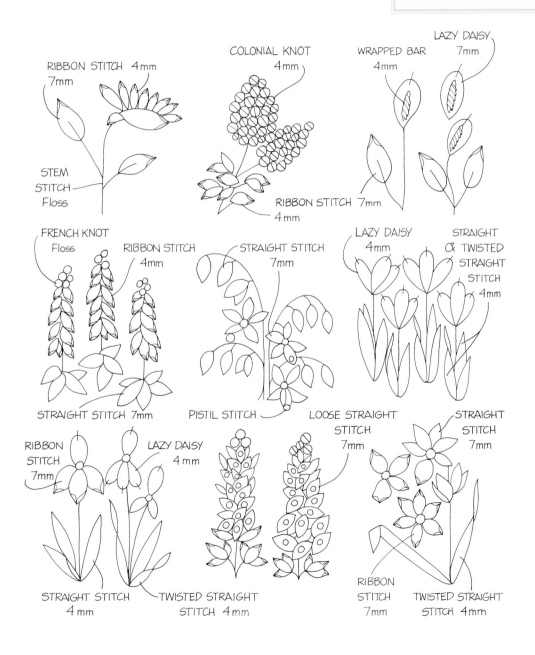

RIBBON STITCH 4mm
7mm

STEM
STITCH
Floss

COLONIAL KNOT
4mm

RIBBON STITCH 7mm
4mm

WRAPPED BAR
4mm

LAZY DAISY
7mm

FRENCH KNOT
Floss

RIBBON STITCH
4mm

STRAIGHT STITCH 7mm

STRAIGHT STITCH
7mm

PISTIL STITCH

LAZY DAISY
4mm

STRAIGHT
& TWISTED
STRAIGHT
STITCH
4mm

LOOSE STRAIGHT
STITCH
7mm

STRAIGHT
STITCH
7mm

RIBBON
STITCH
7mm

LAZY DAISY
4mm

STRAIGHT STITCH
4mm

TWISTED STRAIGHT
STITCH 4mm

RIBBON
STITCH
7mm

TWISTED STRAIGHT
STITCH 4mm

Pillow With Embroidered Letter

Designer: Cathie Bates

*L*IGHTLY MARK THE LETTER of your choice on the doily, then work stem stitch or running stitch over the lines. Work the larger flowers first—the spider web roses, loop flowers, and lazy daisy blooms. Then work the leaves—straight and Japanese ribbon stitch in 4 mm ribbon, straight and lazy daisy stitches in embroidery floss. Scatter French and colonial knots as needed to fill, using 4 mm ribbon and embroidery floss.

When the embroidery is complete, hand-sew the doily to the piece of fabric that will be the front of the pillow, using thread to match the doily. Then make the pillow cover, following the instructions for a flange pillow on page 12.

YOU WILL NEED

FOR THE EMBROIDERY
PURCHASED DOILY WITH LARGE PLAIN CENTER

4 MM AND 7 MM SILK RIBBON

EMBROIDERY FLOSS

CHENILLE NEEDLES

EMBROIDERY NEEDLES

FOR THE PILLOW
PILLOW FORM

FABRIC TO COVER PILLOW

SEWING THREAD TO MATCH DOILY AND FABRIC

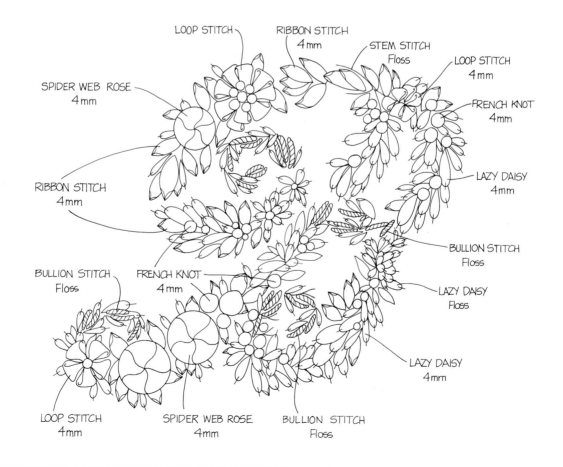

Lined Basket

Designer: Anne Felden

YOU WILL NEED

BASKET WITH HINGED LID

LINEN FABRIC

⅜-INCH (1 CM) BIAS-CUT SILK RIBBON

2 MM AND 7 MM SILK RIBBON

¾-INCH (2 CM) METALLIC RIBBON

CHENILLE NEEDLES

PERMANENT MARKER FOR FABRIC

FLEECE FOR PADDING

PURCHASED LEAF TRIM

WHITE GLUE OR GLUE GUN

EASURE THE INSIDE diameter of the basket lid and cut out a piece of linen about 4 inches (10 cm) wider. Work the embroidery in the center of the linen.

First work the rosebuds in Japanese ribbon stitch, using ⅜-inch (1 cm) bias-cut silk ribbon. To suggest a calyx underneath each bud, make fly and straight stitches in 2 mm silk ribbon. Draw in the stems with a the fabric pen. Add a second cluster of flowers underneath, using Japanese ribbon stitch in 7 mm ribbon and straight stitch in 2 mm ribbon. Use straight stitches of metallic ribbon to create a bow, then draw in the bottom stems.

Cut a piece of fleece the same diameter as the basket lid and place it on the wrong side of the embroidered linen. Wrap the edges of the linen around the fleece and tack the folded linen flaps to the fleece. Then glue the padded embroidery to the basket lid, gluing only the folded area.

Tuck a piece of linen inside the basket to line it and trim the edges down to about 1 inch (2.5 cm). Fold under the extra inch and glue the folded portion to the basket. Cover the fabric edge with purchased leaf trim, gluing it to the linen. Add a sprig of trim to the bottom of the lid.

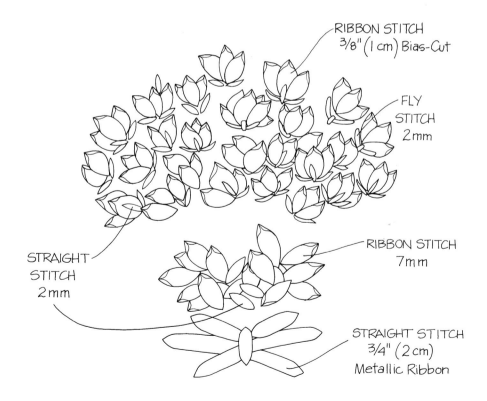

RIBBON STITCH
3/8" (1 cm) Bias-Cut

FLY
STITCH
2mm

STRAIGHT
STITCH
2mm

RIBBON STITCH
7mm

STRAIGHT STITCH
3/4" (2 cm)
Metallic Ribbon

Pillow With Flap

Designer: Ruth Harris

anchor it by making straight stitches across it in matching ribbon. Thread a chenille needle onto one long tail. About ½ inch (1.5 cm) from the bow, make a stitch, then a back-stitch close to it. Continue to tack the ribbon down in a similar fashion, placing your stitches about ½ inch apart and allowing the ribbon enough play to twist and drape gracefully. Repeat with other tail.

Finally, add a fuchsia underneath the bow, using straight stitches for both the body and the petals. Fill in with Japanese ribbon stitches along the cascade. Add stems, pistils, and calyxes in silk buttonhole twist.

*D*ESIGNER *RUTH HARRIS* made a simple pillow from a floral fabric, added a white cotton flap, and worked silk ribbon embroidery in complementary colors. (For pillow-making instructions, see page 12.)

To complete the embroidery, work your way down from the top of the flap, working the larger roses first, then filling in with the rosebuds, leaves, and stems. Add the ribbon stitch flowers and the French knot clusters of grapes.

Now work the bow and cascading ribbon. Cut a long length of 4 mm ribbon. Make a bow in the center of the ribbon, lay the bow on the flap, and

STEM STITCH ROSE 4mm
STRAIGHT STITCH 4mm
FEATHER STITCH Floss
GATHERED ROSE 4mm
RIBBON STITCH 7mm
RIBBON STITCH 4mm
FRENCH KNOT 4mm
RIBBON STITCH 4mm
STRAIGHT STITCH 7mm
PISTIL STITCH Floss
STRAIGHT STITCH 4 mm

Grapevine Needle Case

Designer: Ruth Harris

YOU WILL NEED

FOR THE NEEDLE CASE

DRAPERY MOIRE OR OTHER DRESSY FABRIC

IRON-ON INTERFACING

COTTON FABRIC FOR LINING

FLEECE

THREAD TO MATCH MOIRE

DECORATIVE CORD OR GROSGRAIN RIBBON

FOR THE EMBROIDERY

4 MM SILK RIBBON

CHENILLE NEEDLE

SILK BUTTONHOLE TWIST

EMBROIDERY NEEDLE

BEADS

SEWING NEEDLE

THREAD TO MATCH BEADS

ASSEMBLING THE NEEDLE CASE. Photocopy the needle case pattern as directed and cut it out (or draw your own). Fold a piece of moire in half, place the pattern's dotted line on the fold of the fabric, and cut out the needle case. In the same way, cut out matching pieces of interfacing, cotton lining, and fleece.

Iron the interfacing onto the wrong side of the moire. Work the embroidery on the right side of one end of the moire. (See directions below.) When completed, the case will be folded in half and tied together at the ends.

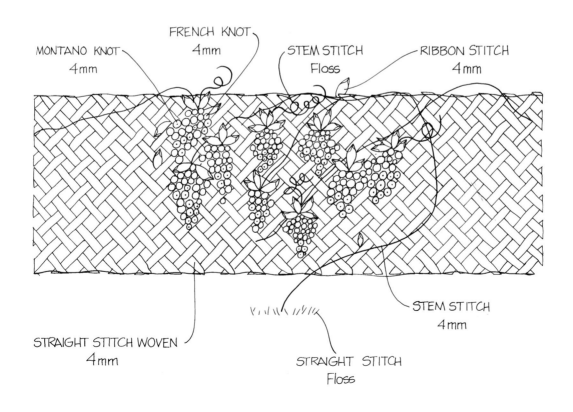

Cut two pieces of decorative cord or grosgrain ribbon 18 inches (45.5 cm) long. Pin one to each end of the needle case, pinning the center of the ribbon to a marked circle. Pin the tails toward the center of the case to keep them out of the way.

Place the embroidered fabric and the cotton lining right sides together. Place the fleece next to the cotton lining, and pin the layers together. Sew around the edge of the case ¼ inch (.5 cm) from the edge, leaving an opening between the notches. Reinforce with extra stitching in areas where the cord is caught in the seam. Trim the fleece from the seam line, close to the stitching. Trim the seam of the lining and moire, but do not trim the decorative cord from the seam line.

Turn the needle case right side out and slip-stitch the opening closed. Topstitch ¼ inch (.5 cm) from the edge around the entire case.

THE EMBROIDERY

Using a pencil and ruler, lightly draw a grid on the right side of the fabric, angling the legs at 45 degrees and spacing them ⅜ inch (1 cm) apart.

Following the grid, make the grapevine trellis. First work all the "legs" that slant in one direction. Each leg is a giant straight stitch; come up at 1, go down at 2, up at 3, down at 4, and so on, keeping the ribbon flat. Then work the legs that slant in the opposite direction, weaving the ribbon over and

under the first legs (see Fig. 1). Sew a bead onto each intersection of the trellis. Outline the trellis in stem stitch.

Work bunches of grapes in French knots. Attach the grapes to the trellis with lengths of grapevine worked in stem stitch. Add leaves of Japanese ribbon stitch and, above and below the trellis, a few blades of grass worked in straight stitch and buttonhole twist.

Figure 1

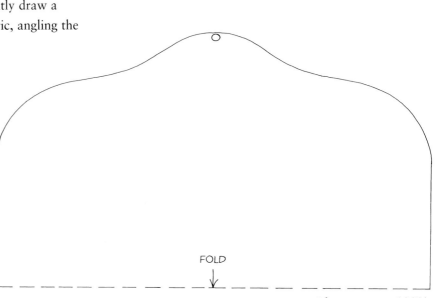

Photocopy at 193%.

Embroidered Hand Towel

Designer: J. Marsha Michler

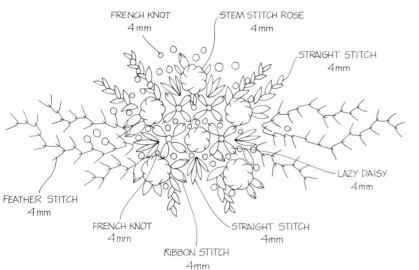

FRENCH KNOT
4mm

STEM STITCH ROSE
4mm

STRAIGHT STITCH
4mm

LAZY DAISY
4mm

FEATHER STITCH
4mm

FRENCH KNOT
4mm

STRAIGHT STITCH
4mm

RIBBON STITCH
4mm

DESIGNER MARSHA MICHLER embroidered a hand towel fit for a guest bath, using 4 mm ribbon exclusively. To make a similar one, first work the stem stitch roses. Next, embroider the French knot centers of the daisies, then make the petals in lazy daisy stitch. Work the foliage in feather stitch and the ferns in straight stitch. Finally, scatter a few French knots over the top of the design to fill.

Heart-Shaped Pillow

Designer: Ruth Harris

CUT A FRONT AND BACK from the pillowcase fabric. (See Making Pillow Covers, page 12.) Complete the embroidery on the right side of one fabric piece. Work the stems in stem stitch, using buttonhole twist. Then work the flowers and leaves. Finally, add the beads and charms. Note that the bird charm carries a bullion-stitch worm; her nest is made of straight stitches and is filled with seed bead eggs. The streamer of twisted organdy ribbon is tacked with beads and sewing thread. At the top of the right side of the heart, there is a cluster of small beads atop larger beads; attach with sewing thread.

Stitch the front and back together, following the instructions on page 12. Hand-stitch the cording around the pillow and tack a tassel at the bottom.

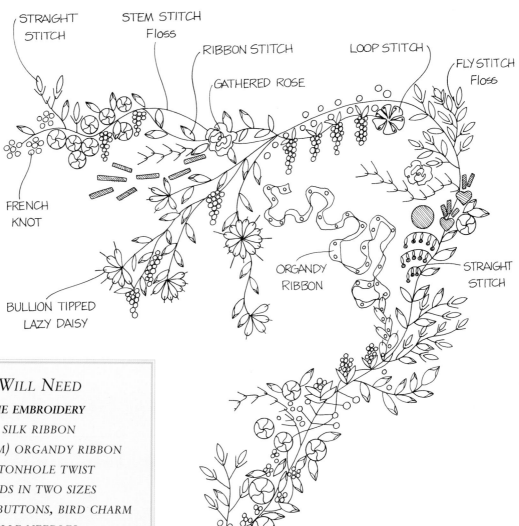

STRAIGHT
STITCH

STEM STITCH
Floss

RIBBON STITCH

GATHERED ROSE

LOOP STITCH

FLY STITCH
Floss

FRENCH
KNOT

BULLION TIPPED
LAZY DAISY

ORGANDY
RIBBON

STRAIGHT
STITCH

SPIDER WEB ROSE

YOU WILL NEED

FOR THE EMBROIDERY

4 MM SILK RIBBON

¼-INCH (.5 CM) ORGANDY RIBBON

SILK BUTTONHOLE TWIST

SEED BEADS IN TWO SIZES

BUGLE BEADS, BUTTONS, BIRD CHARM

CHENILLE NEEDLES

EMBROIDERY NEEDLES

SEWING NEEDLE

THREAD TO MATCH BEADS

FOR THE PILLOW

HEART-SHAPED PILLOW FORM

FABRIC TO COVER FRONT AND BACK

DECORATIVE CORDING

TASSEL

SEWING NEEDLES

THREAD TO MATCH FABRIC,
CORDING, AND TASSEL

Lace and Ribbon Box

Designer: Ruth Harris

YOU WILL NEED

PURCHASED LACE-COVERED BOX
4 MM AND 7 MM SILK RIBBON
DECORATIVE THREAD
GOLD CHARMS
SEWING NEEDLE
SEED BEADS AND BUGLE BEADS
CHENILLE NEEDLES
EMBROIDERY NEEDLES

EGIN WITH THE CONCERTINA rose. Then work the loop flower, the gathered rose, and the Montano knots. Add leaves of Japanese ribbon stitch around the loop flower and lazy daisy leaves under the Montano knots. Work feather stitch and straight stitch in decorative thread, then sew on the charms and the beaded center of the loop flower.

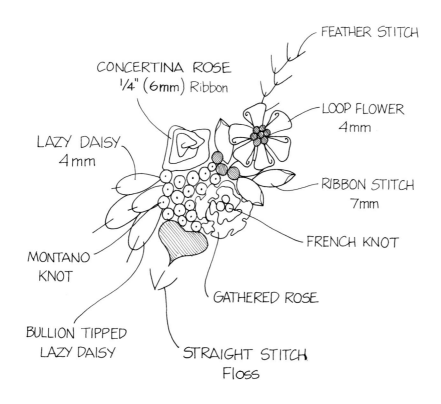

FEATHER STITCH

CONCERTINA ROSE
¼" (6mm) Ribbon

LOOP FLOWER
4mm

LAZY DAISY
4mm

RIBBON STITCH
7mm

FRENCH KNOT

MONTANO
KNOT

GATHERED ROSE

BULLION TIPPED
LAZY DAISY

STRAIGHT STITCH
Floss

Embellished Hand Mirror

Designer: Katheryn Foutz

YOU WILL NEED

PLASTIC HAND MIRROR

¼ YARD *(32 CM)* TAPESTRY FABRIC

¼ YARD FLEECE PADDING

2½ YARDS *(2.25 M)* GIMP
UPHOLSTERY-STYLE TRIM

EMBROIDERY FLOSS

4 MM SILK RIBBON

4 MM RAYON RIBBON

9 MM RAYON RIBBON

7 MM GOLD-EDGED SHEER RIBBON

11 MM ORGANDY RIBBON

CHENILLE NEEDLES

CLEAR GLASS SEED BEADS, BEADING
NEEDLE, AND BEADING THREAD

TAILOR'S AWL *(OPTIONAL)*

FABRIC MARKER

SPRAY ADHESIVE GLUE, HOT-GLUE GUN

ASSORTED VINTAGE BUTTONS

DECORATIVE CORDING

*P*LACE MIRROR ON TOP of fabric and trace around edge with a fabric maker (don't cut it yet). Transfer the design to the fabric. Place the fabric right side up on top of the fleece and hand-baste the fabrics together ⅛ inch (3 mm) inside the traced mirror edge.

Next, make a total of seven ribbon rosettes: three from the 9 mm ribbon, and four from the 11 mm organdy ribbon (one of these will go on the handle).

To make the rosettes, cut the ribbon in 9-inch (23 cm) lengths. Fold one end of the ribbon down at a right angle, with the end extending about ½ inch (1.5 cm) past the long edge to

form a "post" to hold onto. Fold this end in half and stitch securely with thread. Run a gathering stitch along the bottom edge of the ribbon and pull the thread until the ribbon is about 8 inches (20.5 cm) long. Wrap the gathered edge around the post, stitching in place as you go (see Fig. 1). Put the rosettes aside.

Figure 1

To begin the embroidery, make running stitches of 4 mm ribbon on the inner vine where indicated. Whip the running stitches twice, first with more 4 mm ribbon, and then with two strands of floss. Repeat this process for the slightly larger vine outline, using several strands of floss for both the running stitches and whip stitches.

Add leaves in 9 mm ribbon, using Japanese ribbon stitch. Use a tailor's awl, if necessary, to help create an opening large enough to pull these textured and bulky ribbons through the tapestry fabric. Stitch the remainder of the leaves in ribbon stitches, lazy daisy stitches, and bullion-tipped lazy daisy stitches.

Cut a 36-inch (91.5 cm) length of 7 mm gold-edged sheer ribbon, tie a 3-inch (7.5 cm) bow in the center, and pin it in place at the top of the vine design. Tack the bow in place with clear glass seed beads. Thread each bow streamer onto a chenille needle and weave each loosely in and out of the inner vine as shown. Tack down ends with floss.

Add French knots in 4 mm ribbon. Hand-stitch buttons and ribbon rosettes into place.

TO ASSEMBLE

Before cutting out the embroidered fabric, measure the thickness of the mirror. Add that allowance all the way around the outline as you cut (the fabric will fold up over the sides of the mirror).

Lightly spray the back of the hand mirror with spray adhesive and carefully press the embroidered piece onto the mirror. Smooth carefully with your fingers. Clip curves along the edge and glue

down edges with a small bead of hot glue applied to the plastic edge.

Cut a second piece of fabric the size of the handle and glue it to the uncovered side of the handle with spray adhesive.

Hot-glue two rows of gimp trim around the edge of the mirror; make sure the trim covers the fabric edges and the plastic. Next, glue gold cording to the inside edge of the mirror. Be very careful not to touch the hot glue to the mirror surface.

Cover the rough ends of the trim at the base of the mirror with a few simple folded ribbons, a gathered ribbon fan, a rosette, and buttons as desired.

LAZY DAISY

WHIPPED RUNNING STITCH

GATHERED ROSE

RIBBON STITCH

BULLION TIPPED LAZY DAISY

FRENCH KNOT

Sweet Violets

Designer: Patricia Clark

ON THE BACKGROUND *FABRIC*, lightly sketch the lines of the stems and the outlines of the leaves. Make dots where the flowers will go.

Work the stems in stem stitch, using perle cotton. Outline the leaves in buttonhole stitch, again in perle cotton. Next make the violets: two straight stitches in 4 mm ribbon for each petal, and a ribbon French knot for the center. Make buds with two short straight stitches for the petals, straight stitches in perle cotton for each calyx. Finally, fill in the leaves by working ribbon straight stitches between the buttonhole stitches.

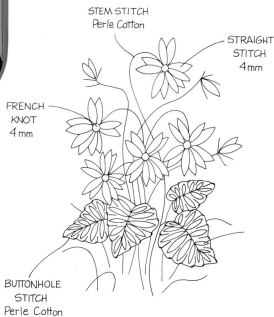

STEM STITCH
Perle Cotton

STRAIGHT STITCH
4 mm

FRENCH KNOT
4 mm

BUTTONHOLE STITCH
Perle Cotton

YOU WILL NEED

BACKGROUND FABRIC

4 MM SILK RIBBON

PERLE COTTON

CHENILLE NEEDLES

EMBROIDERY NEEDLES

Victorian Needle Case

Designer: Joan Toomey

YOU WILL NEED

FOR THE CASE

2 PIECES OF FABRIC 5 X 7 INCHES (12.5 X 18 CM)

5- X 7-INCH PIECE OF VERY STIFF INTERFACING

4- X 6-INCH (10 X 15 CM) PIECE OF FLANNEL (CUT WITH PINKING SHEARS)

FOR THE EMBROIDERY

4 MM AND 7 MM SILK RIBBON

EMBROIDERY THREAD

CHENILLE NEEDLES

EMBROIDERY NEEDLES

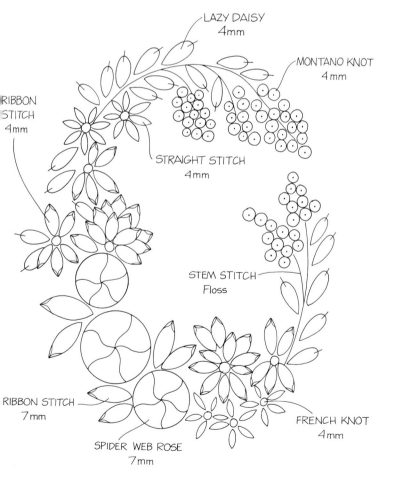

LAZY DAISY
4mm

MONTANO KNOT
4mm

RIBBON STITCH
4mm

STRAIGHT STITCH
4mm

STEM STITCH
Floss

RIBBON STITCH
7mm

SPIDER WEB ROSE
7mm

FRENCH KNOT
4mm

IRST COMPLETE THE embroidery on one piece of the fabric, positioning it as shown in Fig. 1. Lightly draw the oval shape in pencil or erasable marker, to indicate your boundaries. Work the three large roses and the two large daisies, then add leaves, stems, and small knot flowers.

TO MAKE THE NEEDLE CASE

Place the two pieces of fabric right sides together, place interfacing on top, and stitch around the outside edge, using a 1/4-inch (.5 cm) seam allowance and leaving a 2-inch (5 cm) opening along one side. If you like, stitch diagonally across the corners as shown, so that they become slightly rounded when turned. Turn right side out. Fold the case in half with the embroidery to the outside, much like a book cover. Finger-crease the spine gently.

Fold the flannel in half end to end and crease it along the fold. Place the flannel inside the case, matching the two center creases. Stitch the flannel to the case along the creased line, using thread to match the fabric. Stitch the opening closed.

Figure 1

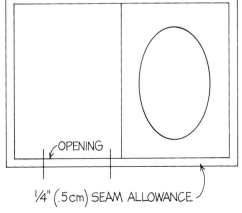

OPENING

1/4" (.5cm) SEAM ALLOWANCE

Round Accent Pillow

Designer: Sara Spiece

*F*IRST WORK FOUR LARGE concertina roses, using the
13 mm satin ribbon. Use a
button, a large pearl, or a group of seed
beads for the center of the flowers. Make
four folded leaves—three from 7 mm satin
ribbon and one from 13 mm—and tack
them around the roses (see directions on
page 63). Work spider web roses in 4 mm
ribbon and clusters of Montano knots in
2 mm ribbon. Work lazy daisy rosebuds
and bullion knots. Then make perle cotton
stems in feather and fern stitch, adding
some lazy daisy leaves. Sew on oval pearl
beads to act as flowers and make a few

straight stitch leaves in 4 mm ribbon.

When the embroidery is complete, assemble the pillow according to the package
instructions.

YOU WILL NEED

*PILLOW FORM AND COVER
WITH BLANK SPACE FOR NEEDLEWORK
(AVAILABLE AT NEEDLECRAFT SHOPS)
4 MM SILK RIBBON
7 MM AND 13 MM DOUBLE-SIDED SATIN
RIBBON
PERLE COTTON
CHENILLE NEEDLES
EMBROIDERY NEEDLES*

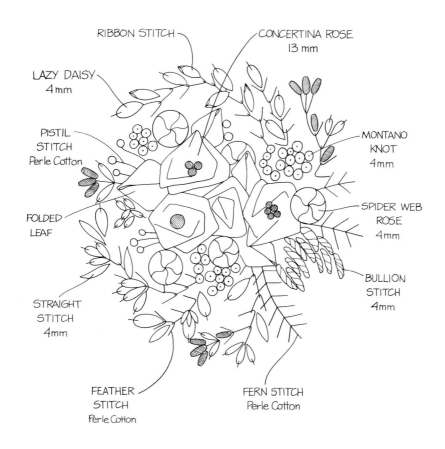

RIBBON STITCH

CONCERTINA ROSE
13 mm

LAZY DAISY
4mm

PISTIL
STITCH
Perle Cotton

MONTANO
KNOT
4mm

FOLDED
LEAF

SPIDER WEB
ROSE
4mm

BULLION
STITCH
4mm

STRAIGHT
STITCH
4mm

FEATHER
STITCH
Perle Cotton

FERN STITCH
Perle Cotton

Scissors Case

Designer: Ruth Harris

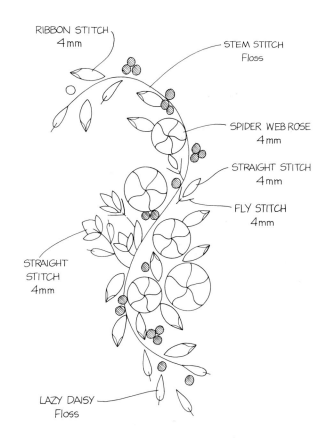

RIBBON STITCH
4mm

STEM STITCH
Floss

SPIDER WEB ROSE
4mm

STRAIGHT STITCH
4mm

FLY STITCH
4mm

STRAIGHT STITCH
4mm

LAZY DAISY
Floss

You Will Need

For the embroidery

4 mm silk ribbon

Silk buttonhole twist

Seed beads

Chenille needles

Embroidery needles

Beading needle or other small-eyed needle

Thread to match beads

For the case

Two pieces of drapery moire or other fancy fabric 5 x 7 inches (12.5 x 18 cm)

Two 5- x 7-inch pieces of muslin

One 5- x 7-inch piece of iron-on interfacing

One 5- x 7-inch piece of fleece

Rattail cording

Thread to match fabric and cording

*P*RESS THE INTERFACING to the wrong side of one of the pieces of moire. Trace the pattern onto the right side of the interfaced piece, centering it more or less. In the traced area, lightly draw a question mark, curving it at the bottom. Using the buttonhole twist, work stem stitch along this line.

Now work the spider web roses and the straight stitch rosebuds in ribbon, with calyxes worked in fly stitch. Using the buttonhole twist, add a few lazy daisy leaves. Sew on beads with sewing thread, scattering them along the main stem.

Cut along the traced pattern line on the embroidered piece. Cut out a second shape from the moire, two shapes from the muslin, and one from fleece. Lay the muslin on the right side of the embroidered fabric; lay the fleece on the muslin. Stitch all layers together, using a ¼-inch (.5 cm) seam allowance and stitching around the broad end between the triangles. In a similar fashion, stitch the other piece of muslin to the right side of the back. Clip at triangles and around curves; turn both pieces right side out.

Place right side of front and right side of back together. Working ¼ inch from the edge, stitch through all thicknesses along the unsewn edge (that is, between triangles on the bottom, narrow end). Trim fleece from the seam. Clip curves and turn case right side out. Whipstitch rattail cording along the outside of the seam.

Letter Sampler

Designer: Cathie Bates

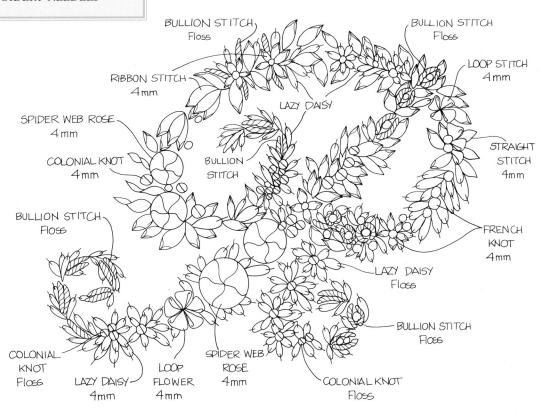

*A*LTHOUGH THIS DESIGNER chose to embroider the letter R, any letter in the alphabet lends itself to similar treatment. Lightly pencil the initial on the fabric and work stem stitch or running stitch over the penciled line. Begin the embroidery by working bullion stitches in embroidery thread at the ends of the letter and work toward the center, embroidering the flowers as you go. After the flowers are worked, go back and stitch the leaves in straight stitch or ribbon stitch, using 4 mm ribbon for some leaves, embroidery floss for others. Finally, work the centers of the flowers with French knots and scatter more knots along the letter, to fill in as needed.

Pin Holder

Designer: Ruth Harris

You Will Need

For the Holder

STIFF MAT BOARD OR POSTER BOARD

SCISSORS TO CUT PAPER

FAILLE FABRIC

BATTING

STRAIGHT PINS WITH DECORATIVE HEADS

For the Embroidery

2 MM AND 4 MM SILK RIBBON

CHENILLE NEEDLES

EMBROIDERY NEEDLES

SILK BUTTONHOLE TWIST

SEED BEADS

C UT TWO 4-INCH-DIAMETER (10 cm) circles of faille; two 3-inch (7.5 cm) circles of mat board; and one 3-inch circle of batting.

Stitch around the edge of each piece of faille, using a large gathering stitch. Pull one of the threads to gather each piece. Place a tagboard circle on the wrong side of each faille piece and turn the fabric edges under the board; gather to fit. Place the batting between the two faille disks. Hand-stitch the two disks together around the edge.

Complete the embroidery on one side. Make the two spider web roses from 4 mm ribbon and a concertina rose in ¼-inch (.5 cm) looped satin ribbon, positioning the three in a rough triangle. Fill in with lazy daisy leaves and decorated lazy daisy flowers. Work a cluster of Montano knots, a spray of straight stitch buds, a group of French knot flowers, and a bouquet of loop stitch flowers with bead centers. Add feather stitches and bouillon knot stitches to fill.

Insert the straight pins around the edge of the holder, inserting them into the batting between the layers of mat board.

FEATHER STITCH Floss

CONCERTINA ROSE ¼" (.5 cm) Looped Ribbon

DECORATED LAZY DAISY 4mm

MONTANO KNOT 4mm

RIBBON STITCH 4mm

LOOP STITCH 4mm

FLY STITCH

FRENCH KNOT

STRAIGHT STITCH

SPIDER WEB ROSE 4mm

LAZY DAISY 4mm

BULLION TIPPED LAZY DAISY 4mm

BULLION STITCH

Christmas Picture

Designer: Sara Spiece

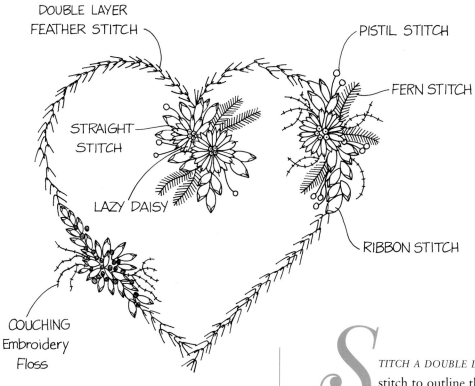

DOUBLE LAYER
FEATHER STITCH

PISTIL STITCH

FERN STITCH

STRAIGHT
STITCH

LAZY DAISY

RIBBON STITCH

COUCHING
Embroidery
Floss

You Will Need

BACKGROUND FABRIC

4 MM AND 7 MM SILK RIBBON

*RAYON EMBROIDERY THREAD OR
PERLE COTTON*

GOLD METALLIC THREAD

*SMALL SEED BEADS AND SEWING THREAD
TO MATCH*

CHENILLE NEEDLES

EMBROIDERY NEEDLES

*BEADING NEEDLE OR OTHER SMALL-EYED
NEEDLE*

STITCH A DOUBLE LAYER of feather stitch to outline the heart. Lightly draw an oval where you want each poinsettia to fall. For each flower, work a circle of straight stitches in 4mm ribbon. Around each petal, work a lazy daisy of rayon thread or perle cotton. Stitch a second layer of ribbon straight stitches over the first, positioning these stitches in the gaps of the first layer. (Don't work lazy daisy stitches for this second layer.) Work yellow-gold Montano knots in the centers.

Work leaves around the poinsettias, using Japanese ribbon stitch in 7mm ribbon. Work similar leaves in a cluster at the lower left of the heart.

With green rayon thread, work the pine boughs, using very fine fern stitches. In the same thread, add couched tendrils as indicated. Work pistil stitches in gold metallic thread. Finally, sew seed beads among the leaves of the lower cluster

Christmas Stocking

Designer: Pat Moore

*D*RAW A FREEHAND *PAPER* pattern for the stocking and cut it out. Lay it on a double thickness of the velveteen and cut out two stocking pieces.

On the right side of one fabric piece (as of now, the front of the stocking), lay out a pattern of lace to create a grid, using different widths and following the prequilted lines in a way that pleases you. Cut each piece of lace so that an inch or so projects beyond the fabric. Stitch the lace to the stocking front with the white thread.

Working block by block in whatever order you like, use the decorative stitching and silk ribbon embroidery to make a memorable stocking. (Glance at your schedule, then decide whether to embellish the back or leave it "plain.")

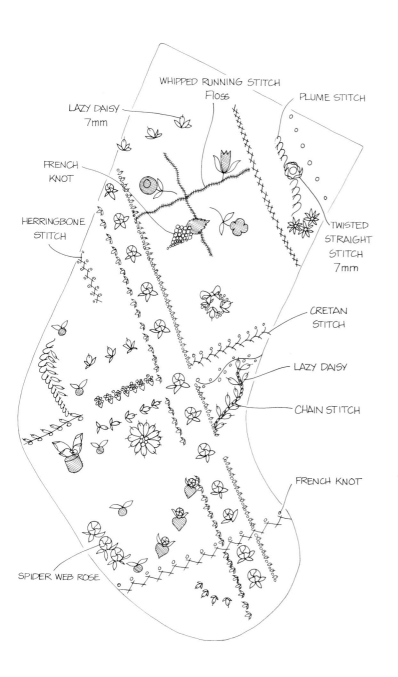

LAZY DAISY
7mm

WHIPPED RUNNING STITCH
Floss

PLUME STITCH

FRENCH
KNOT

HERRINGBONE
STITCH

TWISTED
STRAIGHT
STITCH
7mm

CRETAN
STITCH

LAZY DAISY

CHAIN STITCH

FRENCH KNOT

SPIDER WEB ROSE

YOU WILL NEED

FOR THE STOCKING

PREQUILTED VELVETEEN

PIECES OF LACE ¼ INCH, ½ INCH, AND 1 INCH WIDE (.5 CM, 1.5 CM, AND 2.5 CM)

PAPER AND PAPER-CUTTING SCISSORS

WHITE AND RED THREAD

FOR THE EMBROIDERY

2 MM, 4 MM, AND 7 MM SILK RIBBON

SILK EMBROIDERY FLOSS

SILK BUTTONHOLE TWIST

CHENILLE NEEDLES

EMBROIDERY NEEDLES

Lay the stocking front and back right sides together and stitch around the edge, using a ½-inch (1.5 cm) seam allowance and catching the lace ends in the seam. Leave the top open. Trim the lace ends and turn the stocking right side out. To embellish the top, make a wide piece of lace by stitching three or four pieces of lace together down their long edges. Pin the lace around the top of the stocking. Fold over the top ¼ inch (.5 cm) or so of both stocking and lace, finger-press to crease, and pin in place. Whipstitch the top hem in place.

Crazy Patch
Christmas Ornaments

Designer: Sara Spiece

YOU WILL YOU NEED

*SCRAPS OF SPECIALTY FABRICS
(SUCH AS TAFFETA, VELVET, OR
TRICOT-FUSED LAMÉ)*

MUSLIN (FOR THE FOUNDATION)

*FABRIC IN COMPLEMENTARY COLOR FOR
BACK OF ORNAMENT*

*STITCHING FIBERS (SILK RIBBON,
EMBROIDERY FLOSS, METALLIC THREAD,
AND OTHER DECORATIVE THREADS)*

SEED BEADS

CHENILLE NEEDLES

*EMBROIDERY NEEDLE, BEADING NEEDLE,
OR OTHER SMALL-EYED NEEDLE*

THE CRAZY PATCH. Although Sara Spiece chose a stocking and a heart to grace her tree, you can, of course, make any shape you like.

To begin, draw your desired shape on muslin. Starting at one edge, lay a patch on the muslin and pin in place. Lay a second patch on the first, right sides together. Using a ¼-inch (.5cm) seam allowance, sew the two patches to each other and to the muslin, leaving ¼ inch unsewn at both ends of the seam. Turn the second patch up, press the seam, and pin the patch in place. Continue adding patches in this way until the entire shape is covered. Edge-stitch about ¼ inch (.5 cm) inside the edge all around the shape, then cut it out along the original line.

THE EMBROIDERY

In the style of a crazy quilt, embellish the piece with fibers, silk ribbon, beads, and charms as desired. Do some embroidery along the seam lines and add a few flowers or charms.

FINISHING

Lay the patched shape on the fabric for the back, trace around the shape, and cut it out. Right sides together, stitch around the edge of the ornament, using a ¼-inch (.5cm) seam allowance and leaving about 2 inches (5 cm) open. Turn right side out and stitch the opening closed. Create a hanger for the ornament by lacing a piece of thread through the fabric.

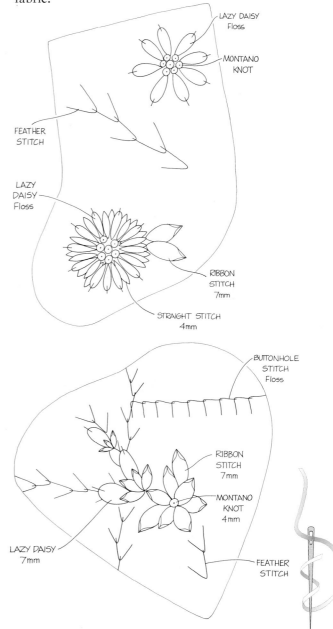

Christmas Tea Towel

Designer: Anne Felden

*F*IRST WORK THE BOW—the vine supporting the leaves and flowers—in feather stitch, using embroidery thread. Using 2 mm ribbon, add the leaves in Japanese ribbon stitch, leaving them somewhat soft and loose. Make one large spider web rose with 7 mm ribbon and two small ones with 4 mm ribbon. Add rosebuds, using 4 mm ribbon and a lazy daisy stitch. At the base of each rosebud, add a fly stitch to suggest the calyx (the green outer petals of the flower), working in silk embroidery thread. To finish, add stems under the flowers, using straight stitches and embroidery floss. Work the French knots in 4 mm ribbon.

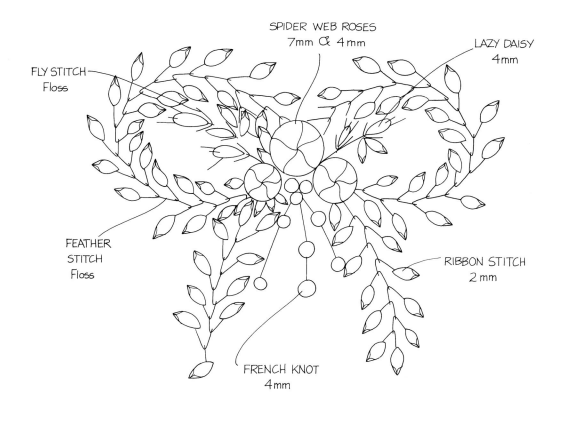

SPIDER WEB ROSES
7mm & 4mm

LAZY DAISY
4mm

FLY STITCH
Floss

FEATHER
STITCH
Floss

RIBBON STITCH
2 mm

FRENCH KNOT
4mm

Shower Invitation

Designer: Anne Felden

YOU WILL NEED

PURCHASED NOTE CARD WITH OVAL
CUTOUT FOR NEEDLEWORK OR
PHOTOGRAPHY

PIECE OF BLACK LINEN TO FIT CARD

ENVELOPE IN COMPLEMENTARY COLOR

4 MM AND 7 MM SILK RIBBON

SILK EMBROIDERY THREAD

SEED PEARLS

CHENILLE NEEDLES

EMBROIDERY NEEDLES

SEWING NEEDLE

WHITE SEWING THREAD

*T*O MAKE THIS MEMORABLE SHOWER invitation, first complete the embroidery on the black linen, then insert the linen into the note card.

Begin with the fuchsias. To make the skirt, cut a 2-inch (5 cm) length of 7 mm ribbon, form it into a circle, and sew the ends together. Run a basting stitch along one edge and pull the threads on each end to gather. Turn the raw top edge over and tack the skirt in position on the linen fabric. Work four Japanese ribbon stitches radiating from the top, using 4 mm ribbon. Each pistil is a straight stitch of embroidery floss with a seed pearl at the tip.

Work all stems in straight stitch, using the silk embroidery thread. Add leaves in loose Japanese ribbon stitches, using 7 mm ribbon, and two flower buds at the bottom, each composed of two Japanese ribbon stitches in 4 mm ribbon.

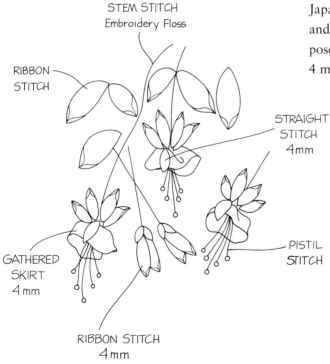

STEM STITCH
Embroidery Floss

RIBBON
STITCH

STRAIGHT
STITCH
4mm

GATHERED
SKIRT
4mm

PISTIL
STITCH

RIBBON STITCH
4mm

Bridesmaid's Gift

Designer: Karyn Sanders

YOU WILL NEED

FOR THE CASE

6-INCH X 4¼-INCH (15 X 11 CM) PIECE OF SILK FABRIC

PIECE OF COTTON FABRIC THE SAME SIZE (FOR LINING)

14 INCHES (61 CM) OF 7 MM SILK RIBBON (FOR TIES)

12-INCH (30.5 CM) PIECE OF LACE

SMALL MIRROR TO FIT CASE (ABOUT 2¼ X 2¾ INCHES, OR 6.5 X 7 CM)

FOR THE EMBROIDERY

MUSLIN

4 MM SILK RIBBON

SILK EMBROIDERY FLOSS

CHENILLE NEEDLES

EMBROIDERY NEEDLES

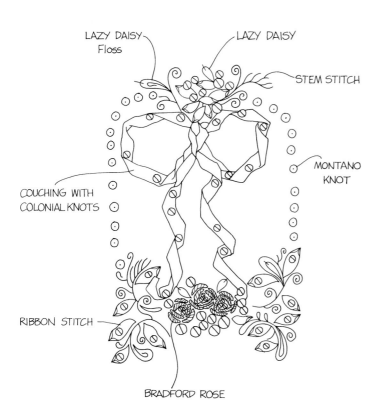

LAZY DAISY Floss

LAZY DAISY

STEM STITCH

MONTANO KNOT

COUCHING WITH COLONIAL KNOTS

RIBBON STITCH

BRADFORD ROSE

*I*NSERT A SMALL MIRROR INSIDE THIS lovely silk case, and you have a fine token of appreciation for a bridesmaid.

THE EMBROIDERY

Cut a piece of muslin large enough to fit into your embroidery hoop and baste the silk piece to it. Complete the embroidery on the right half of the silk, leaving a ¼-inch (.5 cm) seam allowance around the outside edges (see Fig. 1).

First make the bow. Cut a piece of ribbon and tie a bow in the center, twisting the ribbon several times in each loop. Position the bow on the case and pin it in place. Do not pierce the ribbon. Rather, take the pin in and out of the fabric right next to the ribbon, take the pin over the ribbon, then anchor it on the other side in the same way. Lay the streamers in attractive curves, twisting them every inch (2.5 cm) or so. Pin in place. Tack the ribbon to the case with colonial knots in 4 mm ribbon.

Work three Bradford roses at the bottom of the case. Add lazy daisy leaves and colonial knots around them. Work stems and vines in stem stitch and a few leaves in lazy daisy, using embroidery thread. Add Japanese ribbon stitch leaves in ribbon, topping each one with a colonial knot of floss. Work a row of colonial knots around the design, using embroidery floss.

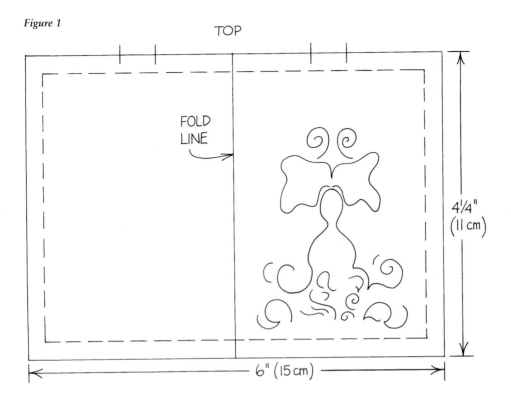

Figure 1

TOP

FOLD
LINE

4¼"
(11 cm)

6" (15 cm)

MAKING THE CASE

Cut the muslin flush with the silk. Run a gathering stitch along one edge of the lace and gather it to fit the top of the case. Sew the gathered lace to the top of the silk, on the right (embroidered) side. Cut the 7 mm silk ribbon into two 7-inch (18 cm) pieces and sew them to the case, on top of the lace (see Fig. 2).

Place the lining and the embroidered silk right sides together, with the lace and ribbons sandwiched between them. Stitch across the top. Fold the pieces back wrong sides together and press. Topstitch the lining to the case along the top, ¼ inch (.5 cm) from the edge.

Right sides together, fold the case in half along the fold line. Stitch the sides and bottom of case together. Zigzag raw edges and turn right side out.

Figure 2

LACE

RIBBON

Bridal Garters

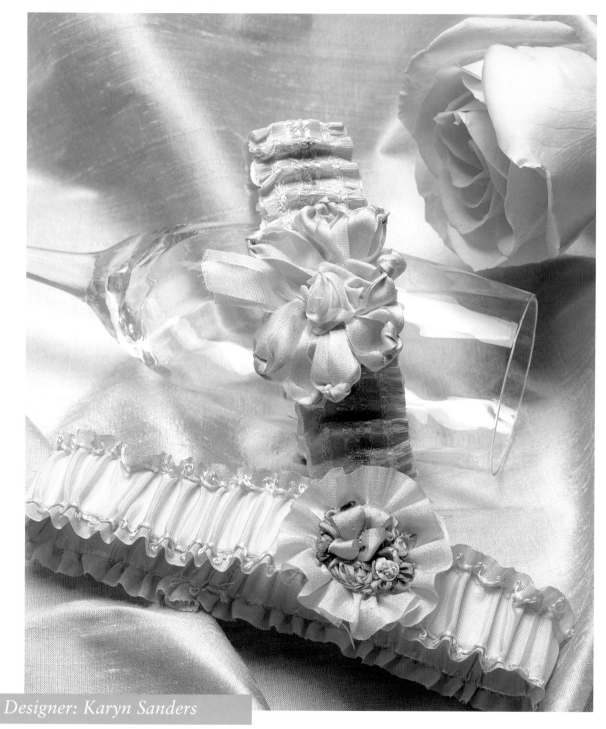

Designer: Karyn Sanders

You Will Need

For each garter

33 inches (84 cm) of fluted or lettuce-edged ribbon 1¼ inches (3 cm) wide

33 inches of 32 mm silk ribbon

elastic ¾ inch (2 cm) wide

For the embroidery
(blue and cream garter)

muslin

7 mm and 13 mm silk ribbon

chenille needles

white glue

For the embroidery
(peach garter) muslin

5-inch (12.5 cm) piece of 32 mm silk ribbon

4mm and 7mm silk ribbon

silk buttonhole twist

chenille needles

embroidery needles

white glue

To make the garters, topstitch the fluted or lettuce-edged ribbon to the 32mm silk ribbon, stitching ¼ inch (.5 cm) from each long edge. Measure elastic to provide a comfortable fit (length will vary), and pull the elastic through the stitched ribbon tube. Pin ends of the tube right sides together, and sew with a ½-inch (1.5 cm) seam allowance. Turn back edges and whipstitch down, for a neat finish. Turn garter right side out.

THE EMBROIDERY

Fit a piece of muslin into your embroidery hoop. In the center, lightly draw a circle about ¾ inch (2 cm) in diameter.

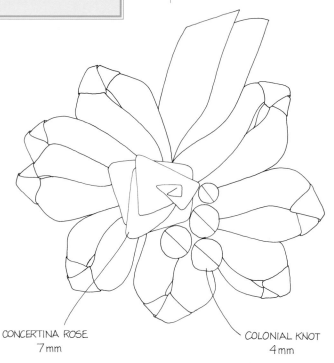

CONCERTINA ROSE
7mm

COLONIAL KNOT
4mm

Blue and Cream Garter

To make the knotted ribbon rosette that graces this garter, first cut eight pieces of 7mm ribbon and eight pieces of 13 mm ribbon 2½ inches (6.5 cm) long. They should be two different colors or shades for the best effect; on the garter shown, the narrower ribbon is blue, the wider one ivory. Put a piece of 7 mm ribbon on top of a piece of 13mm ribbon and tie a loose knot in the center. Repeat for remaining seven pairs of ribbon. With the knot as the center and the 7 mm ribbon facing out, fold ribbon in half and finger press so the ribbon lies flat. Sew tails together, forming a loop. See Fig. 1.

Figure 1

Cut a piece of 7 mm and a piece of 13 mm ribbon, each 1 inch (2.5 cm) long. With the muslin still on the embroidery hoop, pin the ribbons to the muslin so that they project from the circle and suggest the tails of a bow. Trim at an angle.

With knots to the outside, pin the eight ribbon loops to the muslin evenly around the outside of the circle. Place so that the tails from the bow peek out from under the knotted ribbons. Sew ribbons in place.

Work embroidery in the center of the circle: a concertina rose in the center and very loose colonial knots as needed to fill.

Peach Garter

Cut a piece of 32 mm ribbon about 5 inches (12.5 cm) long. Make a running stitch along one edge. Gather to desired fullness and pin in place around the circumference of the drawn circle on the muslin. Sew ribbon ends together and tuck so that they are hidden in the fullness. Sew gathered edge of ribbon securely to the muslin.

Inside the circle, work a loop flower in 7 mm ribbon, then fill in with loose colonial knots, some in 4 mm ribbon, some in buttonhole twist.

FINISHING

On the back side of the embroidered muslin, run a bead of white glue around the outside of the stitching, about ⅛ to ¼ inch (3 mm to .5 cm) from the stitching lines. Allow to dry. (This step is optional, but it will prevent the muslin from fraying.) When dry, carefully cut out the muslin, cutting just outside the glue lines. Either sew or glue the embroidered muslin to the garter, positioning the garter seam in back.

Wedding Album

Designer: Sara Spiece

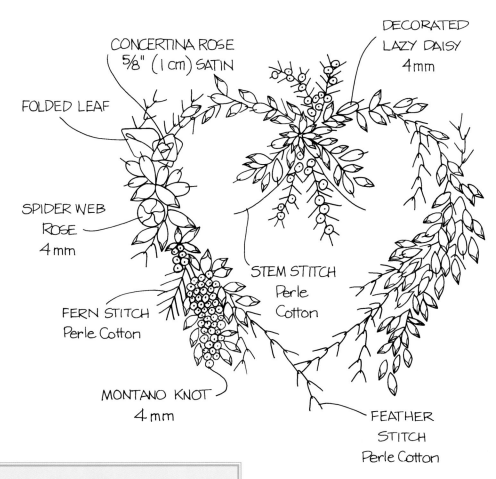

CONCERTINA ROSE
⅝" (1 cm) SATIN

DECORATED
LAZY DAISY
4mm

FOLDED LEAF

SPIDER WEB
ROSE
4 mm

STEM STITCH
Perle
Cotton

FERN STITCH
Perle Cotton

MONTANO KNOT
4 mm

FEATHER
STITCH
Perle Cotton

You Will Need

For the Album

PURCHASED PHOTO ALBUM

BATTING

SPECIALTY FABRIC (SUCH AS TAFFETA
OR SATIN)

FABRIC GLUE OR TACKY GLUE

CARDBOARD OR MAT BOARD

For the Embroidery

4 MM SILK RIBBON

13 MM SILK RIBBON OR ⅝-INCH (1.6 CM)

SATIN RIBBON

PERLE COTTON

CHENILLE NEEDLES

EMBROIDERY NEEDLES

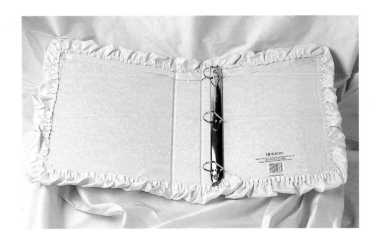

lengthwise and baste ¼ inch (.5 cm) from one edge. Gently pull a thread on each end and gather the fabric. Glue the ruffle to the inside edge of the album. Substitute lace for the ruffle, if you prefer.

Cut cardboard or mat board to fit each inside flap of the album; cut a piece of the fabric about 2 inches (5 cm) longer and wider. Cover the board with the fabric, folding the fabric edges under the board and gluing them in place. Glue the covered boards to the insides of the flaps, securing with straight pins until the glue dries. Replace the inside sheets.

TO WORK THE EMBROIDERY

First work the heart in feather stitch, using perle cotton and adding a few side branches for interest. Make a concertina rose from ⅝-inch (1.6 cm) satin ribbon, a spider web rose from 4mm silk ribbon, and lots of 4mm lazy daisy rosebuds. Work a cluster of flowers in Montano knots and both leaves and flowers in Japanese ribbon stitch, all using 4mm ribbon. Add a branch of perle cotton fern stitch at the lower left.

*T*O COVER THE PHOTO ALBUM, first remove the inside sheets from the album. Open the album so that both flaps are lying flat and lay it on the batting. Trace around the album and cut out the batting so that it fits the outside of the album. Lay the batting on the specialty fabric and cut the fabric about 4 inches (10 cm) longer and wider than the batting.

Place the fabric right-side-down on a flat surface, center the batting on the fabric, and place the album on top of both (still with binder facing up). The album should completely cover the batting and sit in the center of the fabric.

Fold the fabric over the edge of the album and glue to the inside cover. Carefully trim excess fabric around the corners and the ring binder to avoid bulking.

Now make a ruffle. Measure the distance around the outside edge of the album and cut a strip of fabric that's twice this length and 2½ inches (6.5 cm) wide. Fold the fabric in half

Christening Dress & Bonnet

Designer: Karyn Sanders

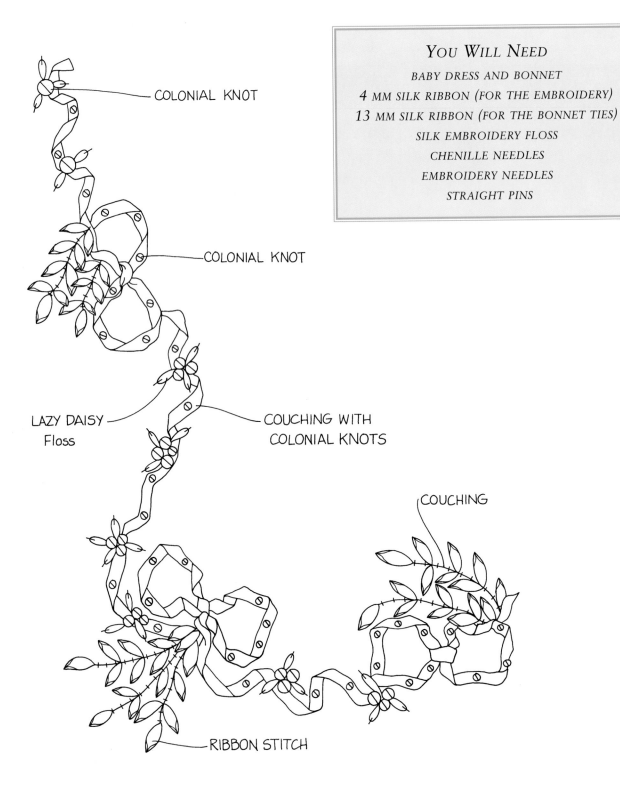

COLONIAL KNOT

COLONIAL KNOT

LAZY DAISY
Floss

COUCHING WITH
COLONIAL KNOTS

COUCHING

RIBBON STITCH

YOU WILL NEED

BABY DRESS AND BONNET
4 MM SILK RIBBON (FOR THE EMBROIDERY)
13 MM SILK RIBBON (FOR THE BONNET TIES)
SILK EMBROIDERY FLOSS
CHENILLE NEEDLES
EMBROIDERY NEEDLES
STRAIGHT PINS

*T*HE PATTERN SHOWN CAN BE repeated any number of times, depending on the size and design of the individual dress. First work the ribbon bows and cascades. Cut a long piece of ribbon and tie a bow in the center, twisting the ribbon several times in each loop. Position the bow on the dress and pin it in place. Do not pierce the ribbon. Rather, take the pin in and out of the dress fabric right next to the ribbon, take the pin over the ribbon, then anchor it on the other side in the same way.

On each side of the bow, lay the ribbon in curves on the dress, twisting the ribbon and pinning it in place. Tie a bow on each side as before, pinning in place. Continue around the dress until you have ribbon everywhere you want it. Then fasten the ribbon to the dress every ½ inch (1.5 cm) or so with a colonial knot of embroidery floss.

Add a spray of flowers to each bow, positioning it in the center of a corner bow, and at the side of other bows. Work the stem first, using couching and embroidery floss, then work the ribbon flowers in Japanese ribbon stitch, leaving the ends of the stitches very loose when you pull them through the fabric.

Along the ribbon cascade, work clusters of three French knots in ribbon. Surround each cluster with lazy daisy leaves in silk embroidery floss.

On each side of the bonnet, work a bow with sprays and clusters of flowers. Cut two long streamers of 13 mm ribbon. Turn under one end of each ribbon and tack it to a side of the bonnet.

New Ways With Silk Ribbon

SMOCKING WITH SILK RIBBON

If you're a smocker, you can create stunning effects by smocking with silk ribbon, rather than with traditional embroidery floss.

You can use the ribbon just as you would ordinary floss in working any of the traditional geometric smocking stitches, such as cable and trellis. (Note the blue taffeta dress at left.) But ribbon's real beauty shines through when you add traditional silk ribbon stitches, such as Bradford roses and lazy daisy leaves. (See the pale green dress at right.)

Ribbon stitches require somewhat different treatment when they are combined with smocking. Most silk ribbon embroidery is done on flat fabric held immobile in an embroidery hoop. In smocking, the design is worked over the hills and valleys of a pleated surface, which expand and stretch. This terrain can prove more difficult to negotiate—but well worth the effort.

Most smockers use 2 mm and 4 mm ribbon; 4 mm ribbon provides the best visual effect. Just about any fabric suitable for smocking will handle pliable silk ribbon; some will handle ribbon far

Three dresses smocked with silk ribbon, all designed by Janice Andrews Balliett.

better than floss. On calicos, for example, floss disappears into the ornate, dense designs, but ribbon stands out perfectly. Unless you use six to eight strands, floss gets buried in napped fabrics such as corduroy and velvet. Silk ribbon sits happily on top.

Tension is a key factor when smocking with ribbon. The looser the tension, the fuller the stitch and the more room it will take up. The tighter the stitch, the more it will resemble floss. As a general rule, keep the stitches tighter on finer fabrics, so the stitch won't overpower the thinner pleats; work looser stitches on bulkier fabrics, to cover the thicker pleats.

If you are a smocker, you must try this!

—*Janice Andrews Balliet*

SILK RIBBON BY MACHINE

While the vast majority of ribbon work is done by hand, Marie Duncan—maverick and committed machine sewer—has adapted the technique to the sewing machine. Rather than threading the ribbon through a needle and taking it in and out of the background fabric, Duncan forms ribbon flowers and leaves on top of the fabric and anchors them in place with machine stitches of invisible thread. For example, to form a bullion knot, she lays one end of the ribbon on the fabric and stitches it down, stopping with the needle in the fabric. She wraps the ribbon around the needle half a dozen times, creating a roll. By hand, she turns the handwheel of the machine to raise the needle out of the fabric. She tips the roll of ribbon on its side and tacks the end in place with a couple of stitches, then sews back to the other end to anchor it. To finish, she cuts the ribbon close to the stitching.

Machine embroidery by Marie Duncan.

Using this technique, Duncan happily turns out looped flowers, French knots, lazy daisy stitches, and more. As someone who prefers the sewing machine, she's faster (and happier) with her contemporary adaptation of an old technique.

CONTRIBUTING DESIGNERS

Janice Andrews Balliett, who likes to combine silk ribbon embroidery with smocking, is the owner of a fabric and needlework shop called The Smocking Horse Collection in Cleveland, Ohio. She has made a how-to video on smocking with silk ribbon, available directly from her (216/235-2035).

Cathie Bates has done all kinds of handwork—crewel, cross-stitch, crazy quilt—but silk ribbon embroidery is her favorite medium because it's "more relaxed and free." Cathie designed and executed the embroidery for the cover of this book.

Patricia Clark is a teacher and designer of quilting and silk ribbon embroidery. A former teacher of home economics and a graduate of Michigan State University, she began her love affair with the needle in early childhood; it continues to be her avenue of communication and expression.

Annette Coan is a painter, computer graphics artist, and needleworker whose silk ribbon wall hangings appear in a number of galleries.

Marie Duncan has worked in the sewing industry for 20 years, during which time she has taught countless people to use sewing machines. She became interested in silk ribbon embroidery when she attended a seminar in which teacher Betty Farrell announced, "This technique can be done only by hand." Duncan's and Farrell's book, *Ribbon Embroidery By Machine,* was published by Chilton Book Co. in 1996.

Anne Felden is a designer and teacher for Lacis, a fine needlecrafts supply company in Berkeley, California. She taught herself silk ribbon embroidery five years ago and has never looked back.

Katheryn Tidwell Foutz delights in ribbons and utilizes them in most of her creations—sewing, needlecraft, fabric sculpting, and floral design. She teaches seminars on ribbonwork and has produced numerous patterns and pamphlets (KTF Designs, 565 Los Osos Valley Rd., Los Osos, CA 93402).

Ruth Harris loves sewing, silk ribbon embroidery, and needlecrafts in general. Having lived in various countries and traveled extensively, she finds that ribbon embroidery is a portable craft.

J. Marsha Michler is a designer for The Magic Needle in Limerick, Maine. She especially enjoys embroidering on purchased items for the home.

Pat Moore has a fine arts degree with a major in art design. She has long had a passion for fine hand sewing and has sewn all her life. She is the owner of Mimi's Fabrications in Waynesville, North Carolina, which specializes in needlecrafts such as quilting and heirloom sewing.

Margaret Pierce is an expert smocker, sewer, and embroiderer. In addition to teaching all three crafts to needlework guilds and craft schools, she owns a mail-order ribbon business (Margaret Pierce, Inc)., in Greensboro, North Carolina.

Karyn Sanders is a self-taught ribbon artist originally trained in costume design. She makes one-of-a-kind wedding gowns and accessories for private clients. Her work has appeared in *Victoria* and *McCalls* magazines. She sells silk ribbon kits through her mail-order business, Sweet Material Things, in Wallkill, New York.

Sara Spiece lives in Grand Haven, Michigan. She works in sales at The Stitching Post in downtown Grand Haven, where she also teaches silk ribbon embroidery, Brazilian embroidery, and quilting.

Joan Toomey started doing silk ribbon embroidery seven years ago. When she couldn't find enough colors of ribbon, she started her own business, Ribbons & Roses. She lives in Herndon, Virginia, and teaches silk ribbon embroidery, quilting, and many other needlecrafts.

Stephanie Williams lives in Frederick, Maryland, where she teaches silk ribbon embroidery. She is particularly interested in antique methods of embroidery, such as gathering and ruching.

ACKNOWLEDGEMENTS

Networking
We'd like to thank all the people who helped us find the silk ribbon embroiderers featured in this book, especially
Pat Moore of Mimi's Fabrications, in Waynesville, North Carolina; Bonnie Benson of Quilter's Resource,
Chicago, Illinois; and Mary Gottelmann of G Street Fabrics, Rockville, Maryland.

Models
Thanks to our models, for showing off the projects to their very best advantage.

Xanath Espina (pages 40 and 65)
Katherine Graham (page 49)
Beverly Jennings (page 32)
Susan Kinney (page 60)
Sally Lee (page 125 left)

Austin Sconyers-Snow (page 36)
Cecelia Thomas (page 125 right)
Mariah Thomas (page 124)
Karla Weis (page 68)
Cindy Wheeler (page 126)

INDEX